Managing the
Day Care Dollars

Managing the Day Care Dollars

A Financial Handbook

Gwen G. Morgan

WHEELOCK COLLEGE

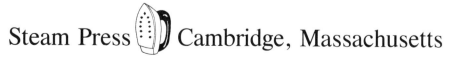

Steam Press Cambridge, Massachusetts

DISTRIBUTED BY GRYPHON HOUSE, INC.

ISBN: 0-942820-02-9
Library of Congress Catalog Card Number: 82-050691

Steam Press
15 Warwick Road
Watertown, MA 02172

Distributed by Gryphon House, Inc.
3706 Otis Street
Mt. Rainier, MD 20712

Additional copies of this book are available through your
local bookstore or educational supply center, or by writing
directly to Gryphon House.

Design by Hal Morgan
Composition by DEKR
MANUFACTURED IN THE UNITED STATES OF AMERICA

Contents

PREFACE

This financial handbook is intended for administrators of local day care and other human service or private education agencies, as a guide and reference to the concepts necessary for good management. The material has a specific focus on day care, but is useful for any administrator who has responsibility for the financial management of an educational organization or one that delivers human services.

The content of the handbook has grown out of sharing among day care directors from all sections of the country who have participated in the Advanced Management Seminars in day care at Wheelock College during the past eleven years. The author is indebted to all those many participants who worked so hard together to develop these ideas and apply them to day care management. I would particularly like to thank two early participants, Nancy Travis and Roger Neugebauer, who continue to be major resources to the field of day care administration, and who continue to share. The Office for Children in Massachusetts has been generous in permitting the reprinting of their *People's Guide to Day Care Accounting* so that it can be more widely used.

Finally, I would like to thank Wheelock College itself, its President, its Graduate School, and its Continuing Education Division, for their steady support in the development of new materials and teaching geared to meet the needs of the resource-needy field of day care, and particularly for their commitment to day care administration at a time when there were almost no other educational programs of this nature for day care managers.

GWEN G. MORGAN
April 1986

Managing the
Day Care Dollars

1. BUDGET IS POLICY

The ability to understand, plan, and control an organization's finances is a central and critical skill. Many directors of human service and educational programs come to these positions through having been skilled in working with children and their families. Without training or experience in financial management, they may believe that they can turn the financial aspect of the program over to somebody else, while retaining control of the program's policy.

Such a belief is totally wrong. There is no way to influence policy without controlling the budget process.

BUDGET IS POLICY.

All our dreams and aspirations for what we want to accomplish for children, for families, for staff, and for the community are expressed in the budget in the language of money. Every line item in the budget is a policy decision which directly determines what the program will be. Whoever makes the budget makes the policy decisions.

This handbook for day care administrators will explain some of the basic tools of financial management which any director needs to be able to use, and which board members should understand.

Who Makes the Budget?

In a corporation, the budget is usually drawn up by the director, sometimes in cooperation with the treasurer of the board, and is then approved by the board. It may be presented to the members of the corporation at the annual meeting.

The director may involve staff and parents in the development of the budget, so that as many people as possible understand the policy decisions that have been made.

In a proprietary (owner-operated) organization, the owner usually develops the budget.

In the case of a new program just starting, the group of people or the individual taking responsibility for getting the program into operation will work out two different budgets early in the planning, in order to be sure that it is feasible for them to start up the day care program. These are the annual operating budget, and the start-up budget.

A new director coming into a program may find that budget information and control have drifted into other hands. An important priority in such a case is to determine at once how the budget is being made, and what skirmishes may have to be fought before the budget process is working as it should in relation to policymaking.

Sometimes a day care program is operating as part of a larger set of activities carried out by a larger organization. In such a case, the budget is made at a higher level than the level of the day care program director, and the process may be a mystery. If the program director is to influence the day care policy, he or she will have to understand the budget as much as possible. The program director will therefore have to seek out the person with budget information, and try to construct, for internal management purposes, a program budget for the day care program.

The budget is not developed by the accountant. Accountants are invaluable to day care programs, but their role is different. Accountants are financial historians. They can track what money came in, and how it was spent, with uncanny accuracy. They can tell you exactly where you stand if you should have to close down the day care program, and they can tell you what you are worth if you need to borrow money. Such information is absolutely essential. You will need an accountant, or accountant services.

But the planning for the future which the budget represents must be done by those individuals responsible for the program's future policy—the owner, the director, and the board, if there is a board. An annual budget is an important document to prepare, because it says to these responsible planners, and also to the outside world, what the program intends to do in the coming year and how it will be able to do it. Both internally and externally, the budget is an important policy statement.

The Budget Process

For a simple day care proprietorship, there should be an annual budget prepared by the owner-operator and any director employed in the program. For a corporation, an annual budget is prepared by the director, and sometimes the treasurer, fully discussed, and formally approved. At the end of the year, a treasurer's report must be prepared to explain to the board how successful the budget was as a plan and a prediction for the year just ended. This year-end report will help in the decisions about the next year's budget.

The budget is most useful if it is treated as an official document, and not lightly departed from. If for some reason things do not work out as planned, and the budget must be departed from, amendments should be proposed to the board and officially approved. This will have to be done if anticipated income does not materialize, since the program cannot stick to a spending plan for money it does not have. An owner of a proprietary day care program should have the same respect for the annual budget, making changes in a formal way. Most experts recommend keeping the original annual budget, even in the face of changed conditions, and simply voting explanatory notes to be attached to explain why the expenditures or income are different than originally planned.

Starting with Two Types of Budget Projections

A budget projection, or a *pro forma* budget, means a best guess about what the budget will be for a specified period of time in the future. For a new program, or for a program adding a new type of service or making a significant expansion, two different kinds of budget projections are needed: the start-up budget, and the operating budget.

The start-up budget includes all the one-time-only costs that are not included in an annual ongoing operating budget—the costs of getting started. It includes the costs of getting a building ready to house a day care program, the costs of planning, and the costs of recruiting and training the new staff. It also expects, and plans for the cost of, a period of under-utilization, during which time the program is not caring for the full number of children it will eventually serve. During this time, the program is not operating efficiently; that is, not operating at its break-even point. This budget must also include some working capital, to cover paying for things before the first income begins, since there is often a time lag between starting and getting paid for the care.

The annual operating budget is a list of all the items on which money will have to be spent once the program is operating at its full planned capacity, with all the planned income coming in, and all the planned expenses going out.

When starting a new program, it is important to make both types of budget at once. It is easy to get bogged down in the time-consuming tasks of planning and meeting the start-up expenses. Since start-up comes first, and presents many major obstacles, its problems loom large. But it is a very serious mistake to embark on start-up expenses without a very firm plan for where the operating money is going to come from. Start-up may be difficult, but these costs are insignificant when compared with the day-in and day-out costs of operating a program over the long haul.

Start-up costs should not be included in the first year's operating budget, because they would inflate that budget beyond a feasible limit. It would then be impossible to figure how to price the service offered.

An operating budget and a start-up budget are presented in the next section. For directors or board members who have never constructed a day care budget, these budgets can be used as exercises for developing the budget skills essential for these roles in the day care organization.

The newcomer to budgeting will not get very far with the tasks of constructing a budget without encountering a number of prior decisions that have to be made about the program before a number can be entered in the budget. All these decisions will turn out to be policy decisions about the program. Making a budget with several people will involve making agreements about policy decisions. There is no quicker way to find out that budget is policy than to put together a budget for the first time.

Two Sides to a Budget

A budget always has two sides. There is the income side, which documents all the sources of expected income, and the expenditures side, which documents all the expected expenses for the year. These are two different aspects of the plan for the year. It should be obvious that if one side changes, the other must change, too. If the income side turns out to be less than expected, then the plan for spending will have to change at once, so that the program is not spending money it does not have available to spend. If the expenditures turn out to be greater than expected, then more money will have to be found, or spending changed in some other part of the budget.

Some Crude Rules of Thumb for Planning

There is no such thing as a day care cost in any absolute terms. Your costs are determined by what you must spend, as required by law in the licensing requirements or as required in the specifications of any public funding source, by what you decide you want to spend, and by what you have available to you to spend.

Your costs and sources of income will have to be carefully worked out in your budget. Before making the budget, it may be helpful to think about costs and their feasibility through some crude planning formulas.

Richard Ruopp offers a quick way of guessing at the order of magnitude of your day care center's costs:

First, ask yourself what you think a classroom teacher should be paid, on average. Second, ask yourself how many children a classroom teacher should be responsible for (the ratio of children to staff). Third, divide the amount a classroom teacher should get paid by the number of children. Fourth, multiply that number by two, since classroom staff are about half the total budget of a day care center, with the other costs coming from administration, supplies, equipment, the building, and other costs.

The formula is:

$$\frac{\text{Salary of one teacher (annual)}}{\text{Number of children/staff}} \times 2 = \text{cost/child/year}$$

That is, a center that pays its teachers $12,000 on the average to be responsible for eight children needs an income of $3,000 per child per year.

Day care is expensive. If the day care program intends to operate with a heavy dependence on parent fees, an analysis must be made of costs to determine whether parents can afford to pay the fee. After you have made your annual operating budget, the annual expenditures should be divided by the number of children expected, to get a rough per child cost. The actual cost will be a little higher than this figure, since the program cannot operate at 100% enrollment all the time.

Unless all the parents are at upper income levels, they probably cannot afford to pay more than 10% of their total gross family income for day care, even if they have more than one child. If most of the parents who will be using the program earn incomes less than ten times the per child cost of the day care expenditures side of the budget, then the program will either have to seek sources of subsidy to supplement what parents can pay, or else change its plan for spending.

Ten percent of family income is suggested as a very crude rule of thumb for planning. Very rich parents could undoubtedly afford to pay 15% of their income for child care, but few are likely to be willing to do so. Poor parents, however, cannot pay as much as 10% of their income for child care; they have trouble making ends meet with their payments for food and shelter. Another crude rule of thumb that might be used is that families earning less than half the median income for a family of four are not able to pay more than a small token amount for their child care.

Median incomes for a family of four are available each year from the Secretary of Health and Human Services, for use by the states in determining their definitions of eligibility for subsidized day care. The national median is around $20,000. State medians for 1982 follow, although of course day care planners will be most interested of all in the expected incomes of the families that live near the program they hope to operate.

A final crude rule of thumb for planning is the size of the expenditures for different parts of the day care budget. A study was done in 1970[1] of twenty exemplary day care programs that examined the relative percentage of the day care budget for six different functions. Although the level of expenditure may be very different today, the percentages spent on different aspects of day care may be quite similar. The study found:

Child Care and Teaching	70% to 37% range	50% average
Administration	27% to 8% range	16% average
Feeding	19% to 6% range	11% average
Health	14% to 0% range	4% average
Occupancy	22% to 9% range	13% average
Other (transportation, social services, etc.)	23% to 0% range	6% average

---

1. *A Study in Child Care, 1970–1971* (Cambridge: Abt Associates, April 1971), Table IV, p. 20.

Although these costs vary greatly, depending on the availability of free or low cost services in some cases, they do give some guidance. For example, if the cost of a building and utilities under consideration were 25% of a total planned budget, it is likely that the program might not be able to survive, since that is far beyond not only the average, but also the top of the range of costs in these programs studied.

MEDIAN INCOME FOR FAMILIES OF FOUR FOR FISCAL YEAR 1982

State	Income	State	Income
Alabama	$18,613	Montana	$20,051
Alaska	31,037	Nebraska	20,749
Arizona	23,000	Nevada	25,457
Arkansas	18,493	New Hampshire	22,335
California	25,409	New Jersey	24,640
Colorado	25,228	New Mexico	21,032
Connecticut	24,410	New York	21,082
Delaware	21,184	North Carolina	19,648
D.C.	21,310	North Dakota	19,520
Florida	20,757	Ohio	22,528
Georgia	21,578	Oklahoma	20,852
Hawaii	24,582	Oregon	24,031
Idaho	24,265	Pennsylvania	22,314
Illinois	22,567	Rhode Island	21,636
Indiana	22,614	South Carolina	20,154
Iowa	22,567	South Dakota	19,209
Kansas	22,648	Tennessee	19,437
Kentucky	19,138	Texas	23,416
Louisiana	20,166	Utah	21,250
Maine	18,074	Vermont	19,314
Maryland	24,686	Virginia	22,976
Massachusetts	23,786	Washington	24,410
Michigan	24,422	West Virginia	18,876
Minnesota	24,409	Wisconsin	23,518
Mississippi	17,672	Wyoming	22,673
Missouri	21,294		

A Budget Checklist

Before you make the budget, you will need to have the following information:

A. Staff

____1. Budget salaries for all personnel positions, whether full time or part time. Don't forget office staff, maintenance, snow shoveler, cook, and anybody else who will be on your payroll.

____2. Budget for raises, if you intend to be able to raise pay.

____3. Budget substitute time whenever regular staff will not be in the classroom, including sick leave, vacations, compensatory time, and work release time for training.

____4. Remember that Social Security is required by law; currently 7% is contributed by the employer and 6.7% by the employee.

____5. Workmen's Compensation rules differ from state to state; it is probably required by law if you have ten or more employees. Check with an insurance agent.

____6. Check unemployment laws. All fringe benefits are subject to change.

____7. Decide what total benefits you will offer staff on your payroll.

____8. Decide what benefits will be given to substitutes and budget separately.

B. Consultant and Contract Services

____1. Decide what consultants you will employ: doctor, dentist, psychologist, nutritionist, training specialist, outside speaker.

____2. Decide what services you will use instead of staff: cleaning services, accountant services.

____3. Include the cost of movies for in-service training, and attendance at workshops and conferences.

____4. Include the cost of subscriptions, books, and memberships in organizations like Day Care Council of America, state Day Care Associations, and early childhood professional organizations.

C. Occupancy

____1. Include rent or mortgage payment. Check to see if any changes are coming up next year.

____2. Budget for maintenance of building and grounds, including some regular schedule of repair and upkeep. Use prior records if available, and allow for rising costs.

____3. Budget for fuel, light, and water. Check on possible rate increases.

_____4. Check with the telephone company to see if they expect a rate hike.

D. Supplies and Equipment

_____1. Include here all materials that will not last longer than a year—things that will be consumed or used up.

_____2. Include different kinds of supplies: classroom, kitchen, laundry and housekeeping, and medical supplies.

_____3. Don't include capital costs for start-up. Do budget in the operating budget for a planned five-year schedule of replacement costs of equipment.

E. Other

_____1. In figuring transportation costs, include vehicles, gas, oil, tires, and repairs.

_____2. Check with your insurance representative to see if insurance rates are going up.

_____3. Remember costs of license, building approvals, and related costs.

_____4. Include a small miscellaneous account to cover unanticipated costs for items that do not fit into other categories. Petty cash is not a budget item.

_____5. Include in your operating costs any repayment you will have to make for loans from a bank or other sources to start up your program.

THIS IS A SIMPLE, LINE-ITEM BUDGET FOR ANNUAL FULL OPERATION OF A CENTER

Annual Budget for Fiscal Year _____
Face Sheet

INCOME:

Fees from parents   _____
Fees from Title XX   _____
Registration fees   _____
Special fees and sales   _____
Transportation charges   _____
USDA Food Program   _____
Payment from other government sources   _____
Gifts, contributions, and fund raising   _____
    Restricted to specific uses   _____
    Unrestricted   _____
Investment income   _____
Loan received   _____
Sale or exchange of property   _____
Miscellaneous   _____

TOTAL INCOME   _____

EXPENDITURES:

Personnel   _____
Fringe benefits, payroll tax @ 12%–15%   _____
Special fees, contract services, and consultants   _____
Supplies   _____
Occupancy   _____
Furniture, equipment, and vehicles   _____
Conferences, workshops, and special events   _____
Other expenses   _____

TOTAL EXPENSES   _____

Number of children, full time   _____
Number of part-time children that together add up to full-time equivalent (enter FTE number)   _____
Total number of expected children   _____

TOTAL PER CHILD COST   _____

Note: You will adjust this budget's expected income by a utilization factor.

This is a Budget Back-up Sheet for the Line-item Budget

1. EXPENDITURES FOR PERSONNEL

Title	Name	Salary/mo.	% time employed	Annual pay
List administrative/clerical staff				
List classroom staff (use additional page if necessary)				
List social service staff				
List domestic/maintenance staff				
List health staff				
Cook				

TOTAL STAFF _____

2. FRINGE BENEFITS

    Federal witholding   _____

    State withholding   _____

    FICA   _____

    Workmen's Compensation   _____

    Bonding insurance   _____

    Health insurance   _____

    Other fringe benefits   _____

               TOTAL FRINGE BENEFITS   _____

VALUE OF DONATED SERVICES, CETA STAFF   [_____]

               TOTAL PERSONNEL COSTS   _____

3. PROFESSIONAL FEES, CONTRACT SERVICES, AND CONSUL-
TANTS

    Maintenance contract   _____

    Catered food   _____

    Transportation, portal to portal contract   _____

    Health services, contracted or consultant   _____

    Training services, contracted or consultant   _____

    Legal services   _____

    Accounting services   _____

    Other   _____

      TOTAL PROFESSIONAL FEES AND CONTRACTS   _____

        Value of donated professional services   [_____]

4. SUPPLIES

    Teaching and child care   _____

    Food supplies, kitchen supplies   _____

    Office supplies   _____

    Housekeeping supplies   _____

Building, grounds, and maintenance supplies   _____

Health supplies   _____

Vehicle supplies   _____

Other consumable supplies   _____

TOTAL SUPPLIES   _____

Value of donated supplies   [_____]

5. OCCUPANCY

Rent   _____

Real estate taxes   _____

Maintenance and repairs   _____

Amortization of leasehold improvements   _____

Utilities   _____

Building insurance   _____

Interest on mortgage (if building owned)   _____

Depreciation (building only)   _____

Other building occupancy costs   _____

TOTAL OCCUPANCY COSTS   _____

Dollar value of donated space or land   [_____]

6. FURNITURE, EQUIPMENT, AND VEHICLES

Purchases of furniture, equipment, and vehicles; or rental or installment payments

Office furniture and equipment   _____

Building equipment   _____

Teaching and child care   _____

Kitchen   _____

Vehicle   _____

Other   _____

Depreciation on furniture, equipment, and vehicles   _____

Maintenance and repairs

  Office furniture and equipment   _____

  Building equipment   _____

  Teaching and child care   _____

  Kitchen   _____

  Other   _____

Other   _____

TOTAL FURNITURE, EQUIPMENT, AND VEHICLES   _____

Dollar value of donated furniture, equipment, and vehicles   [_____]

7. CONFERENCES AND WORKSHOPS, SPECIAL EVENTS AND
   SERVICES

Expenses (food, transportation, babysitting, etc.) for
board meetings, advisory groups, community relations,
fund raising   _____

Expenses for conferences and workshops for staff   _____

Fees or transportation for family services outside center _____

Expenses (food, transportation, babysitting, etc.) for
parent social activities, parent conferences, parent
education   _____

Special events, services, field trips for children   _____

Other   _____

TOTAL SPECIAL EVENTS   _____

Dollar value of donated goods and services   [_____]

8. OTHER EXPENSES

   Advertising, printing, and duplicating (outside) _____

   Telephone and telegraph _____

   Postage and mailing _____

   Professional memberships _____

   Bank charges, loan payments, interest _____

   Licenses and permits; transportation insurance _____

   Uncollectable accounts (bad debts) _____

   Contingency fund, payments into _____

   Loss from fire, theft, or vandalism _____

   Indirect administrative expense of parent organization,
   franchise, or corporate expense where applicable _____

   Other _____

   TOTAL OTHER EXPENSES _____

   Dollar value in-kind donations (describe) [_____]

   GRAND TOTAL ALL EXPENSES _____

   GRAND TOTAL DONATED VALUE [_____]

Budget Justification

A budget justification is a narrative description, line by line, of the reasoning that led you to arrive at the figures you are using. Some of the information you will be presenting in the budget justification, if you make one, includes the following:

1. *Personnel.* List all your staff, by title and name, if they are already employed, as follows:

Executive Director Jane Jones @ $1000/mo. (100% time) $12,000 annual

If you are starting a new program, you may not know exactly what each employee will earn, and you will budget a salary *range*. If you are running an existing program, you will know what salaries staff are getting, but you will budget for salary increases according to some predictable schedule, which you will attach.

Budget substitute time for all positions that require substitutes, and explain the basis for your estimates. Remember that substitutes are needed when your regular staff are sick, on leave or vacation, have compensatory time off, or have released time for training. You may also want to plan for substitutes if a staff person should leave suddenly, although that seldom happens if your policies are clear.

You may want to budget substitutes in the third section of the budget, under Contract Services and Consultants rather than here, because you may not pay fringe benefits to substitutes. If you pay some, but not all, benefits to substitutes, include them here.

2. *Fringe Benefits.* Do not include employee contributions in the budget. There are two kinds of fringe benefits: those that are freely offered by the center and included in the contract with the employee, and those that are required by law, or mandatory.

Non-mandatory benefits include:

(a) The amount of the center's expense for the employee's life insurance or retirement plan, if any. Programs are able to make certain benefits available to employees on a group basis. It is customary for employers to share in the cost of such insurance, making a contribution that matches the employee's contribution. Many day care centers have not had sufficient incoming funds to make such a contribution. Some of these centers have nevertheless been able to make these benefits available to employees who wish to pay the full cost at the group rate, rather than having no insurance plan. Budget only the employer's contribution, not the employee's contribution.

(b) The amount of the program's expense for the employee's health benefits, usually Blue Cross/Blue Shield or another health plan. This will be explained in the justification in this type of form:

Health Insurance @ $10/mo./person × 8 employees × 12 mo. = $960

(c) The center's expense for any other non-mandatory employee benefits.

Mandatory benefits include:

(a) The Federal Insurance Contributions Act (FICA) is a payroll tax, which is voluntary for new not-for-profit organizations. Once the decision is made to join, the program becomes mandatory.

FICA is based on a percentage of each person's salary as the employer contribution. Do not budget the employee matching contribution. An entry might look like this:

FICA @ 7.51% x $50,000 salaries = $3755

(b) Unemployment Compensation is mandatory. Check in your own state for the provisions. An employer may choose to pay in advance a regular amount, or pay themselves for all claims from former employees, essentially insuring themselves. The Workmen's Compensation Plan is therefore a kind of insurance plan to cover against claims that an employer must honor in any case. Check with your insurance agent on what is required in your state, and what the percentages are, since these are subject to change. For example, Workmen's Compensation covers day care center employees in Massachusetts or Georgia, if you have ten or more employees. Employers may choose to pay in advance a percentage of each employee's salary, part of which would go to the state and part of which would go to the federal government, in advance, to cover claims that might be made.

Check carefully on all fringe benefits each year, since they are subject to change in cost and in percentages required. Once you have the information, you will probably be able to work out a rough percentage of salaries for estimating all fringe benefits, such as fifteen percent, which you would explain in the justification. This permits quick computations.

Apply this kind of quick computation only to those employees who receive all the benefits. You might have to figure substitutes and part-time employees at a different rate. This, too, you would explain in the justification.

3. *Professional Fees and Contract Services.* In this final section of your personnel section you include all services provided by people not on your regular payroll, either consultants or services you are securing by contract or on a retainer basis. These would include fees for speech and physical therapists and curriculum specialists; payments made to doctors, nurses, dentists, hospitals, and clinics; and all fees for professional consultation in administration, accounting services, training services, legal services, and the like. Transportation for field trips is not included here. Substitutes are usually budgeted in this section, unless the center pays fringe benefits for substitutes. There are no fringe benefits for contract services and consultants.

4. *Supplies*. This part of the budget covers all materials that will be totally consumed or will not last longer than a year, and equipment that costs less than $250.

5. *Occupancy*. This section explains all costs arising from a program's use of a building and land, and all donations of space and land. If a center pays rent, it may have certain utility costs in addition to the rent, or these costs may be included in the rent. If a center owns a building, it may have mortgage payments and real estate taxes. These costs will be explained in this section of the justification.

Maintenance and repairs covers all payment to outside vendors, but not to center staff, for repair maintenance, gardening, snow removal, rubbish removal, window washing, painting, plumbing, carpentry, dry cleaning of drapes, rugs, and furniture, repair or maintenance of furnace and boilers, and minor building improvements.

Utilities covers payments of electricity, gas, oil, and water, but not the telephone.

Building insurance covers all insurance associated with building occupation, including fire, wind, burglary, and public liability insurance.

Depreciation is the cost of a building and maintenance or repair in excess of $250, all of which may be depreciated to reflect the decline in value over time. The Federal Internal Revenue Service has regulations for computing depreciation, with expected useful lives which are allowable for different large items of equipment. Depreciation is not important for tax-exempt organizations.

Amortization of leasehold building improvements is a way of spreading the costs of major building improvements (more than $250) over a period of several years.

Other occupancy costs include amounts of less than $250 for window washing, waste and rubbish removal, snow plowing, dry cleaning, and the like.

Donated space means the fair market value or rental value of donated property, *or* the excess of such fair value over the rent actually paid.

6. *Furniture, Equipment, and Vehicles*. This budget section covers equipment that will not be used up in a year, in contrast to the supplies covered in section 4. In this section you will budget replacement costs on equipment that will break down during the year. The initial new equipment to start the center off should have been in the start-up budget, or somehow amortized beyond the first year. This item covers the costs necessary to replace such equipment on a regular schedule.

Depreciation may be budgeted over the useful life of the item, using IRS guidelines. Not-for-profit organizations usually do not figure on depreciation, since the tax advantage does not benefit them. Instead they plan a five-year cycle so that the same amount is being spent each year to replace different things, to prevent expenses from bunching up in the same year.

For-profit organizations should figure the depreciation on their equipment. Do not use replacement cost (or new equipment cost) for fair market value.

7. *Special Events and Services.* This section includes the expenses for various meetings and events, exclusive of staff costs that are budgeted in the personnel sections. Expenses for parent development, staff development, board development, field trips, and other meetings and events are budgeted here.

8. *Other Expenses.* When budgeting for telephones, remember installation costs. Check with the telephone company, your insurance agent, and others about possible increases. Enter the amount of loss from fire, theft, or vandalism if you encounter such loss, whether or not there is insurance payment to cover the loss. The insurance payments to you will be reported as income. Shop for the best liability insurance rates since they are completely unpredictable at this time.

Some programs, particularly those that are sub-parts of a larger organization such as a college or a multi-service agency, also include an indirect cost figure to cover the overhead costs to the parent organization, such as bookkeeping, payroll, fund raising, oversight, maintenance, utility costs, and the like. The federal government will conduct an audit to establish an indirect cost figure if a program is going to conduct a federally funded program for the first time, and this cost figure will then be fixed, governing future federally funded projects.

Also under "indirect expense" should be listed any payments to franchise holding companies or corporate expense.

In-Kind or Donated Goods and Services. The budget guides on the preceding pages include space for figuring the value of donated aspects of the day care program, even though these do not represent actual cash expenditures or cash income. These aspects of the day care program's budget will not affect pricing, and are therefore included within parentheses wherever listed.

There are many reasons why the day care operator, the funding source, the parents, and the general public should have access to knowledge of all the different resources that a center has. For one thing, it is not possible to compare costs from one center to another unless there is complete information about all the resources as well as money that a center is using.

For purposes of determining the cash costs of a program, these items should not be added in. For purposes of determining the true value of the program, they should be added in.

An in-kind donation is any goods or services donated to your child day care service. It means anything of value that is used by the program in providing its service, that was not purchased out of the budget, or any services performed by a person not on the payroll.

Ideally, you will know what your in-kind aspects of the budget are, so that you can demonstrate the value of the service you are providing, and the true costs of providing it. In-kind can include any of the following:

- Food donated by a parent, volunteer, or friend for a party, picnic or special occasion

- Art supplies, toys, equipment donated by friends or community groups

- Toys donated to be given to the children as Christmas or birthday gifts.

- Clothing given the center to be distributed to the children

- Visits by the librarian for story hour

- Vision, teeth, sickle cell screening

- Regular volunteers, who should sign in

- Services rendered by a parent or a friend: repairing toys, painting walls or furniture, cleaning up play areas and the like

- Services rendered by a parent or a friend: emergency plumbing or electrical repairs, heating, etc., at which a person is expert

- Services rendered by a parent or a friend: typing, bookkeeping, tele-phoning, carpooling, etc.

- Services rendered by a parent or a friend: sewing curtains, making equipment, rebinding blankets, etc.

- Services rendered by parents, friends, volunteers: story-telling, as-sisting with field trips to zoo, beach, museum, etc.

- Visits by groups to entertain children: puppet theatre, Girl Scouts, Boy Scouts, singing groups, etc.

- Visits by children to the fire house, barber shop, museum, etc., if someone at these places has taken time to explain his occupation or act as guide to the children, and/or if there is usually a fee to get in, but it has been waived

- Time spent by parents in planning, activities, and fund-raising

- Time spent by the director and staff over and above the regular work day, without additional pay

A donation, to be included, should meet the following criteria:

- It should have a measurable market value.

- It should serve a useful function to the center.

- It should be furnished directly to the center, and under the center's administrative control, rather than routinely provided as a public service, as for example, a public health visiting nurse.

For example, when a parent who works in an interesting place which charges a fee to the public for entrance offers to get all the day care children in free, that is a donation, and its value will be the fees which the center would have had to pay without the parent's offer.

Include as donated services the dollar value of labor of all persons who provide specialized services to the center and who are qualified professional practitioners. Public, tax-supported health services such as a public health nurse, or free consultation from the nutrition department of the state, are not donated services, since they are paid for in another budget. Contributions of personal services can be computed on the basis of the value of the time contributed, whether at the minimum wage or at the going rate in the community, for the type of specialist donating the time in their specialization.

HOURLY RATES FOR SERVICES 1982

Accountant/Auditor	$ 9.00	Painter	$11.50
Bookkeeper	5.00	Physician	25.00
Bus Driver	5.50	Plumber	12.00
Carpenter	12.00	Professor	12.00
College Instructor	7.50	Policeman	10.00
Cook	5.00	Psychologist	15.00
Dance Instructor	7.00	Recreation Worker	4.00
Dentist	20.00	Secretary	6.00
Dietician, Nutritionist	7.00	School Administrator	12.00
Education Specialist	10.00	Social Worker (MSW)	7.50
Electrician	13.00	Social Worker (other)	5.50
Janitor	5.00	Speech Therapist	10.00
Lawyer	20.00	Swimming Instructor	5.00
Music Teacher	7.00	Teacher (Elem./Second.)	6.00
Nurse, RN	7.00	Therapist/physical	10.00
Nurse (other)	6.00	Typist	4.50

2. STARTING UP: THE INITIAL COSTS

Starting a new day care program, or starting a new component added to an existing program, involves a number of costs that must be met before any operating money begins to come back in. These costs include:

- Capital costs of building, land, and equipment

- Human costs in planning, getting a program ready, securing a license, recruiting children and staff, and starting off with fewer children than capacity for the first several months

- Lag costs, since there is a substantial time gap between providing the service and getting it paid for, particularly if government funds are involved. You may have to pay your creditors before your creditors pay you.

- Miscellaneous other costs. There may be other costs, such as public relations, professional fees to lawyers and accountants, and license and building approval fees.

It is important to anticipate these costs as much as possible, even though they vary greatly. Plan for a cushion against unanticipated costs.

Each of the items in the budget has a range of potential costs. Sometimes you will not be making the expenditure at all. If you find space that needs no renovation, for example in space that was formerly already used for day care, or that was designed for this use, you may not have to spend money for renovation. You might feel you could get along with little or no staff training in advance of beginning the new program if money is tight and if you employ experienced staff.

You may meet some of the costs through in-kind contributions. Perhaps the person starting the new program is an energetic parent able and willing to donate a lot of time to the start-up activities. Perhaps staff will be willing to put in a little of their own time before the pay period starts. Perhaps you can get shelves, equipment, cubbies, and chairs built for much less than they would cost if you bought them, or you may get some useful donations.

Finally, in practice, you can push some of these costs over into the first year of your operating budget by not paying some bills until the money starts to come in, although the more of this you do, the more you inflate your

THIS IS A START-UP BUDGET FOR A DAY CARE CENTER

Year _____

INCOME
    Bank loan _____
    Gifts and contributions _____
    Fund-raising events _____
    Other _____

                             TOTAL INCOME _____

EXPENDITURES	Cash	In-Kind	Amortize
Personnel			
Person who plans and implements start-up period	_____	_____	XXXX
Staff employed before children are enrolled	_____	_____	XXXX
Fringe benefits @ 12%–15%	_____	XXXX	XXXX
Contract services and consultants			
Architect	_____	_____	_____
Lawyer	_____	_____	XXXX
Renovations, contractor	_____	_____	_____
Other	_____	_____	_____
Supplies	_____	_____	_____
Occupancy			
Rent or mortgage payment	_____	_____	_____
Deposits	_____	XXXX	XXXX
Utilities	_____	XXXX	XXXX
Furniture, equipment, and vehicles	_____	_____	_____
Training of new staff	_____	_____	XXXX
Board meetings, parent meetings	_____	_____	XXXX
Other			
License fee	_____	XXXX	XXXX
Insurance	_____	XXXX	XXXX
Publicity	_____	_____	_____
Payment into cash reserve	_____	_____	_____
Other	_____	_____	_____

CASH NEEDED FOR TOTAL EXPENDITURES _____

operating costs beyond the point that income can sustain them. Sometimes you can amortize a cost over a longer period of time, such as leasehold improvements made by a landlord.

Day care administrators are known to be skilled mobilizers of people and scroungers of resources, and nowhere is this talent more needed than in the start-up period. Many people in the community will need to be involved, in most cases, before the program gets off the ground, its license in hand, its building equipped, and its finances sound. In addition to scrounging resources that are donated, the program will need some cash on hand to cover its operating expenses before income begins to flow.

Start-Up Analysis

Personnel costs: Decisions must be made about who is responsible for all the start-up activities, whether a volunteer or a paid person. In large urban areas, it can take six months to a year to get a day care program incorporated, building approved, licensed, and ready to operate. Even if someone is spending this time without being paid, it must be decided at what point the paid director is employed and starts to work, or in the case of a proprietorship, how long the owner can finance the program out of pocket without any money coming in.

Most administrators starting a new program would prefer to employ a full staff, and train them together as a team before any children enter. In practice, however, it is usual to compromise this ideal in the interest of cost feasibility, and to phase in the hiring of staff to match the very gradual rise of children over time, since programs seldom reach their full capacity in a short time.

Contract Services and Consultants: You may employ a lawyer to help with incorporation, tax status, and other legal aspects of start-up. Such help could cost at least $100, and could easily cost much more. Free or reduced cost help might be available from a Legal Services agency or from a parent or friend.

In cities, you might have to employ an architect to draw up plans to submit for building safety approval and zoning. These fees can be $300 to $400 or more, even with little design help, and are not usually required in smaller communities.

Any help you need to pay for in advance of starting, from educators, doctors, nutritionists, psychologists, or other day care experts, if not available free, will have to be budgeted.

Supplies: These are an operating expense after the program is under way. You may want to purchase at bulk rate more supplies than you can use right away, and in any case your initial expense of purchasing everything is probably going to be greater than it will be in subsequent months and years. If you defer purchase of supplies to the point when the center is almost ready to begin, and spread the purchases out over the year, you can avoid major start-up costs for supplies. You may want to finance some supplies as part of start-up.

Occupancy: You will want to start occupying your building *at least* one month before you enroll children in order to get ready. Utility companies, the telephone company, your landlord, and other services may require deposits of various amounts before the program begins.

The selection of your building is probably the most important decision that you will make. Your payment for rent or mortgage is buying you two things: a place to run your program, and advertising.

Remember: Occupancy costs are a combination of space and advertising.

Before selecting the location, you will have gathered information on community resources that can help your parent group, on other competing day care programs, and on parents' need for day care and their ability to pay. A well located program, in an area of need, that is visible in the community, will reach and maintain its break-even point much more readily than a program that is not well located and visible. There are some locations where you will never break even.

Besides the decision of where to locate the day care program, you will have to decide whether to build, renovate, or find an existing program that needs no renovation (a former day care program, school, or hospital).

You will also decide whether to own the building, and pay mortgage, or whether to rent.

All these decisions have different cost implications, and you may need to pay for expert advice. Remember that your operating budget will not be able to sustain costs of occupancy that are too large a proportion of your overall costs, certainly not as much as 25%.

In most states you will be required to have 35 square feet of usable space for each child, as part of the licensing requirements. Most day care centers meet this requirement with 60% of their space, using an additional 40% of space for storage, kitchen, offices, hallways, entrances, and meeting space. You can figure on needing at least 40% more space than the 35 square feet per child.

Multiplying the number of children you expect to have by 35 will give you the square footage you need for 60% of your building. The calculation[1] of total space needed is as follows:

$$\frac{35 \text{ sq. feet}}{60} = \frac{X}{100} \text{ or } .6X = 35 \text{ sq. ft. or } X = 58.33 \text{ sq. ft. per child}$$

---

1. *Day Care Financial Management: Considerations in Starting a For-Profit or Not-for-Profit Program* (Save the Children Child Care Support Center, January 1981).

These are minimum figures, of course, and an ideal program would have more space. But with this calculation, you can estimate the number of square feet you will need for the number of children you want to include, and multiply it by square footage costs for building or for renting buildings in the local area you are considering.

The total land area for a 60-child center has been estimated at 250 square feet per child, including building space, outdoor play areas, and areas of driveways and sidewalks. Therefore an average land cost *if $1 per square foot* could be roughly $250 per child, and that could be multiplied by the number of children. If parking spaces are required, additional space should be added. Construction costs vary considerably over time. If they are $40 per square foot, the overall cost of building would be $40 times 58.33 square feet, times the number of children; plus $250 times the number of children; plus the cost of parking space.

Renovation costs vary from nothing or very little all the way to a cost close to that of new construction. If the building has not previously met a building code for day care, a school, hospital, or similar use, it is likely that changes have to be made to meet the requirements for building safety approval, and for sanitation approval, both prerequisites to the license. These changes are likely to include protection for the furnace or boiler, additional exits, fire resistant doors, and kitchen and bathroom equipment. A frame house may require extensive renovation to make it safe from fire dangers. A store front may require major renovations; a single width storefront will cost $5000 to $10,000 to renovate for 25 children.

When there is a Housing Authority or Redevelopment Authority, it is sometimes possible to get rent-free space for day care programs. Churches have classrooms that are often only used on Sunday, and which may not require much renovation. It is usually unwise to spend more than $10,000 to renovate an old building, although there are no hard and fast rules.

If you are renting the building, the landlord will either make the needed improvements and charge you for them over a long period of time, or try to recapture them more quickly through high rent. In some cases, you can work with a friendly landlord to get the renovating done with volunteers and in other low-cost ways. Since there are many ways that landlords can handle these costs, you will want to discuss your financial situation quite fully with potential landlords, and find the landlord you can develop the best working relationship with.

Furniture, Equipment and Vehicles: Some furniture and equipment can be built in and amortized with the renovation costs. Equipment costs will vary widely. Initially, you will need equipment costs of around $300 to $400 per child, including kitchen equipment, educational equipment, maintenance and housekeeping equipment, office equipment, and medical equipment. Of this, more than half is kitchen equipment, and about one quarter is educational and medical equipment.

Initial expenses for kitchen equipment can easily run $6,000 to $8,000. Food money from the United States Department of Agriculture, administered by the Bureau of Nutrition, in most states' Department of Education, was formerly available for this purpose, but may be cut. Other than that, public funds are not available for equipment or other start-up costs, although government surplus equipment may be used.

Training: A new program may hire its core staff, a little in advance of opening, bearing in mind that full staffing is not possible until enrollment is secure enough to justify it. An intensive orientation/training period the week before opening will help the staff operate as a team. However, this is a costly practice for a center without access to much start-up capital. Decisions about the number of staff to be employed before there are children, and the timing of their hiring, will seriously affect start-up costs. For this reason many cautious operators phase in new staff as they phase in children, allowing for unanticipated delays in enrollment.

If there are training costs, they will also be budgeted in this section.

Meetings: Any expenses entailed in meetings of parents, planners, or staff, or transportation to visit other programs or go to meetings, should be estimated.

Insurance: You can probably include these costs in your operating budget, but they will be incurred before you begin. Check for most recent prices and shop around for the best price.

Publicity: Money spent on making the new program visible is worth the investment if done in a way that has been demonstrated to bring in new day care children. New programs in day care usually have longer start-up periods than were anticipated. It takes a long time before full capacity is reached. The longer the time, the more costly the operation and the more risky the endeavor. It is very important to use every creative way possible to let the community know of the new service, and help to build trust in its quality.

For this reason, you will want an attractive sign, one that is in keeping with the style of the neighborhood in which you are locating. Your outdoor play equipment, in areas of low vandalism, is a part of your attractiveness. Open houses, newspaper stories, hand-out flyers, posters in supermarkets and laundromats and churches, raise the level of information about your service in the community. An attractive ad in the Yellow Pages has been demonstrated to have a high return. Mailings are expensive, and are probably not worth the investment, unless you can persuade your bank or other community merchant to include your flyer in another mailing.

Repayment of Loan: If you have borrowed money in order to start your center, you will include any interest payments and the repayment of principal in your operating budget. The justification will explain as follows:

Loan Repayment—Annual Payment on $20,000 Start-up loan: $5000

Cash Reserve: If you deal with government funds for the children participating in the program, you will have a serious cash flow problem. It will take the government a long time to process your bills and reimburse your program for its expenses. You will usually have to pay the bills you owe before the government pays you what it owes you. It is absolutely necessary to have enough money on hand on opening day to cover your operating expenses for a while. The more you receive from the government, the longer this cash reserve should stretch. Some experts say you need three months' operating expenses; others say more, and some say less. You can offset some of these cash flow problems, and protect yourself against bad debts at the same time, by asking for a deposit of at least one week's fees from all your parents. You can also charge an enrollment fee, for families you accept and those on your waiting list. But even with these practices, you should be prepared for the need for working capital in reserve.

Sources of Start-Up Funds

Parents can pay some initial deposit that will help with the need for working capital. Usually, there is a need for substantial other funds. There is no government source of such start-up capital, not even for not-for-profit services.

Not-for-profit programs find their start-up funds through seeking either foundation grants or loans. Sometimes local foundations are willing to help with start-up, if they feel the program has demonstrated a capacity to meet its operating costs after the start-up period. Loans can be secured from individuals or from banks. In the case of loans, the program has to find a way of repaying the loan in the future, and therefore these costs have to be amortized into the operating budget. Obviously, foundation grants would be preferable.

In the case of for-profit programs, the larger chains have ways of recapturing the start-up costs in the real estate transaction, in sale of stock, and economies of scale in equipment. This handbook does not deal with these larger operations, but with the small proprietor owning or running a local operation. For-profit operators can secure a loan from the Small Business Association or from a bank. Or they can cover the costs through adding equity to their own or someone else's investment in this start-up period.

Whether the needed cash comes from a loan or grant, in the case of a not-for-profit operation, or from equity or a loan, in the case of a for-profit operation, they almost always involve someone else's money. These other sources of funds are not readily available to programs that appear unlikely to survive the start-up period. Fifty percent of all businesses fail in the first two years. Bankers and investors, as well as foundation decision-makers, will be looking for evidence of sound financial planning before they will part with their money.

Making a Financial Plan

An outline for a financial plan that would be likely to result in a loan from a bank or individual, and a proposal for a start-up grant would be very similar. Both would include:

COVER SHEET: Name of organization, names of principal planners, address, and phone number.

STATEMENT OF PURPOSE: The purpose of seeking the financial help should be described.

SECTION I.   THE PROGRAM: This section describes the purposes of your organization and why it will be successful. It describes the target families that will use the program, the location selected, needs in the area, any competing services, the experience and competence of the principals, how the loan or investment or grant will be used, its effect, and a brief summary. This is a most important section for a foundation, where the concern is for the value as well as the competence of the undertaking.

SECTION II.   FINANCIAL DATA:
A. A budget, with sources of operating funds. Face sheet. Back up.
B. Capital equipment list (Omit for new programs.)
C. Balance sheet
D. Break-even analysis
E. Income projections (Take budget face sheet, and project summary for three years, in three columns.)
F. Projected cash flow, by month for one year
G. Deviation analysis (existing program only)
H. Historical financial reports (existing program only)
   1. Balance sheet for last year, add columns for past three years if available
   2. Income statements for past three years if available
   3. Tax returns for for-profit organization
   4. Tax-exempt documentation for not-for-profits

SECTION III.   SUPPORTING DOCUMENTS: Add personal resumes, letters of reference, copies of leases, contracts, IRS tax exemption for not-for-profit organization, and anything else relevant to the plan.

Most day care directors have had little practice in using these tools themselves, much less demonstrating their competence in using them to bankers and other sources of funds. Except for Section H, the information should be prepared primarily by the director, and not turned over to an accountant.

Assuming that the program has been able to secure start-up funds, and has its operating budget under good control, these financial planning skills will be required of the director to keep the program in good working order, and of any new director entering the program in order to understand and guide its future.

The remainder of this handbook is geared to helping the inexperienced day care administrator master the basic useful ways of preparing and presenting information to help a program survive and accomplish its goals.

3. THE INCOME SIDE OF THE BUDGET

It should be clear after creating a line item operating budget and a start-up budget that all budgets consist of two balanced sides: the money coming in and the money going out. These two sides must be the same.

Income is always related in some way to the numbers of children enrolled in the center. If the center gets a government subsidy, it is usually for purchasing care for a particular number of children. If parents pay fees, the amount of the fees collected is dependent on the numbers of children enrolled.

Utilization Rate

In the simple case of a center entirely financed by parent fees, the entire income side of the budget is based on the numbers of children and the fees paid for each of them. In first planning a budget you are likely simply to multiply the numbers of children expected to be enrolled by the fees they will pay. However, that is a serious mistake in planning. You will overestimate income, and your planned expenditures to match your expected income will then be greater than the income which actually does come in. You need to determine a *utilization rate*.

Unless you over-enroll, it is not possible to operate a program at 100%

enrollment. When children leave, others will not always take their place on the same day. A well run center operates at above 95% enrollment, but a few programs achieve as high a rate as 98%. Careful attention to attendance records to be watchful that non-attendance is not turning into non-enrollment, quick action to fill empty slots from a waiting list, and recruitment activities to build good community relations even when all slots are filled, will assure that utilization does not fall to 90%. But to anticipate income accurately, it is important not to anticipate 100% enrollment. New programs may well be operating at 80%. Income based on fees will be:

No. of children × fees per child × utilization rate

Your utilization rate is your best estimate of the percentage of children who will actually be enrolled over the course of the year as compared with full enrollment at capacity.

For example, if your maximum capacity is 50 children, and your fee is $200 per month per child with reduction for holidays, illness and vacation, then the maximum you could earn in fees would be $200 × 12 (months) or $2400 per year for each of the 50 children. Your maximum income from fees would be $120,000. If you budget to spend that much, however, you will run out of money, because that is not your expected earnings. If you examine your records and find that your actual earning in fees for the previous year was $114,576, then that figure is more likely to be your earnings this year, given the same capacity, or number of children possible to enroll.

Your utilization rate for the year would be the $114,576 actual earnings from fees last year, divided by the maximum, $120,000. This figure, .955, is your utilization factor, expressed in a percentage as 95.5%.

If your utilization rate is lower than 92% after several years, you are probably not monitoring enrollment to operate at an effective level. You will therefore probably want to try to increase your utilization rate through better management of attendance reporting and recruitment of children.

The above example was a very simple one for a center operating entirely on parent fees, with no sliding fee scale, and no part-time children. Part-time children need to be estimated by adding them up to full-time equivalent children, in whatever way reflects the fees charged them. In general, two half-time children cost more than one full-time child, and should be charged more than half if fees are to reflect costs.

If parents pay a sliding fee, and the government pays the other portion of the sliding fee, the calculation can be made by combining what parents pay and what government pays into a total fee for that child, as follows:

No. of children × (parent fee + government subsidy) × utilization rate

Note that the calculation was again very simple because it was again assumed that parents were going to pay for all days, including holidays, illnesses, vacations, and the like, and it was further assumed that the policy of the government about whether they would pay is the same as the policy of the parents. Those are reasonable assumptions, but they may not be correct. They are reasonable, because expenses of the center will continue on those days, so there is certainly a need for income to come in to cover those expenses. Centers that charge on the basis of attendance, rather than enrollment, must cover these costs in another way, by charging high enough fees to cover the costs of these expenses. The calculation above assumes that the center is charging a full fee for all days, whether or not the child is there, with income based on enrollment, adjusted for actual enrollment rather than maximum potential enrollment. Probably the most sound policy would be to set fees in the expectation of a certain number of holidays per year, and a two-week vacation that is not paid, since most people will follow that pattern. The fees for the rest of the year would be great enough to cover the paid holidays by staff, and the unpaid vacation of the children. The important point to make is that the center should know and plan what its policy is about enrollment, attendance, vacations, and holidays, when it sets its fees.

If the day care program is financed through Social Service Block Grant Funds from the state, state policy will determine the basis for payment, whether enrollment, attendance, average annual enrollment (as described above), or some other formula. States have policies which often penalize centers for periods of low attendance, as a way of promoting enrollment efficiency. Regardless of state policy, the budget used for management should project a true picture of projected fee income through use of a utilization factor. An alternative permitted in some states, but not others, is to overenroll by the number of children expected to be absent, a practice which reduces the gap between enrollment and maximum enrollment at the same time that it increases the number of children in attendance.

Note that attendance and enrollment are not the same thing.

A program can be fully enrolled and operating efficiently in relation to enrollment, and still go through periods of low attendance because of a measles epidemic. There is no way a day care program, or any similar educational program such as a dancing class, a typing class, or a college class, can adjust its expenditures to reflect variations in attendance, and that is why payment based on attendance destroys the stability of a program. Programs can, and do, base expenditures on expected enrollment, and adapt their expenditures to shifts in enrollment.

Another factor that affects income projections is the impact of bad debts, which will vary from program to program. If a center has a history of a large number of bad debts, then probably the fee collection policies are not adequate, since it is possible to run a day care program with very little bad debt. You will need to improve your fee collection procedures, but take into consideration the past experience of losses in trying to project income.

Monitoring Enrollment and Attendance

There are many ways of anticipating income and expenses in relation to numbers of children: attendance, enrollment, average attendance, or average annual enrollment. The most useful for program management is average annual enrollment. Unfortunately, many states reimburse on the basis of attendance. Even if paid on the basis of enrollment, there are many problems.

For centers that operate in crowded urban areas, with long waiting lists, there is no recruitment problem, but they will have to keep careful track of attendance to be sure a child is not in the process of dropping out without informing the director. Someone should be examining attendance records weekly. Since the income projection is based, in one way or another, on numbers of children, then every child lost will be a serious reduction in income.

The number of children per staff person (ratio) is the central factor in day care income and expenses. If you have budgeted 12 three-year-olds and two staff people, and if for some reason you decide to accept an extra child whose family needs the service badly, you will find yourself with plenty of leeway to buy what you need all that year. If, on the other hand, you have budgeted for twelve but can only find eleven children to enroll in the three-year-old group, you will be losing money rapidly and endangering the whole program. You may cut the napkins in half and water down the poster paints to no avail. The problem is in the ratio. Only one child will make a tremendous difference. Whenever a child leaves, then every week that goes by without filling the space is a threat to the survival of the program.

In the less densely populated areas, the monitoring of attendance to assure continuing full enrollment is even more critical. With a less substantial pool of children from which to draw, as compared with urban areas, the center may be faced with extinction in times of recession if very many families lose their jobs and cannot continue the child care. It becomes a vital issue to keep the entire community aware of the existence of the program, and to use every public relations technique possible to be sure that the entire pool of families in the area knows about the program. In these areas, too, the day care program needs to serve a wide range of needs because the area will be less likely to support several specialized programs to meet different needs.

It is clear that attendance records, usually combined with fee records, are among the most important of financial management records, and that the information they contain should be examined frequently, and acted upon at once.

Opposite is a weekly record of attendance and fees. The following two pages are a monthly record of attendance and fees.

44

WEEKLY SUMMARY OF ATTENDANCE, AMOUNTS DUE AND CASH RECEIPTS

Name of child	Rate	M	T	W	T	F	Amount Due This Week	Balance From Previous Week	Received This Week	Adjust-ments	Balance Now Due

Explanation
of Adjustments _____

_____

Center Director's   Social Worker's
Signature _____   Signature _____

                        Wk.   Deposit
Center_____ No._____ End_____ Date_____ No._____

Finance Department Copy   Canary=Center Copy   Pink=Audit Copy

45

MONTHLY RECORD OF ATTENDANCE AND FEES

Date _____ (month)

Name of child	M	TU	W	TH	F	Fee	M	TU	W	TH	F	Fee	M	T

1 = sent first notice after one week in arrears
2 = sent second notice one week later
3 = sent termination warning one week later
4 = sent termination notice one week later

/	TH	F	Fee	M	TU	W	TH	F	Fee	M	TU	W	TH	F	Fee	1	2	3	4

Recruitment of Children

Recruitment of children is almost synonymous with good community relations. Public relations, described earlier in the start-up budget section, will be a continuing need for any program that does not have an ample and self-generating waiting list. Even with a waiting list, some centers still make efforts to be visible, as a hedge against shifting economic conditions of the future.

Some programs depend on recruiting parents that can afford to pay; and others have contracts with the state for children eligible for subsidy. Regardless of whether the parents or the state pays, it is a good idea for programs to make sure that the families in the community know of the program, rather than relying on referrals from the local welfare office or from the state. In some cases, these referrals may not reliably keep the spaces filled. You cannot afford to let much time go by with unfilled spaces in day care, when the income side of your budget has counted on this subsidy fee. It is better to be sure by taking the responsibility yourself for community relations.

The best sources of recruitment do not cost much money, although they may use valuable time. They include spending time on the telephone with parents seeking services, even when there is no room, in order to retain good will of the community. They include word of mouth among the friends, relatives and neighbors of parents using your program, visiting referral agencies in the community, and visiting employers' personnel departments. Word of mouth has been found to be the most effective of all methods of recruitment, so that it is worth time and effort to increase the information being circulated around the community in this way.

The next most effective method of recruitment is the Yellow Pages. An ad placed here has a much higher return than one placed in the newspaper. Other good methods are the development and distribution of brochures, and giving them to real estate agents, pediatricians, people who visit your center, churches, libraries, health departments, information and referral services, schools, and above all to your parent group to distribute. Similarly, bright and creative flyers can be tacked up in the same places, and in supermarkets and laundries. Someone in a day care center is sure to have an eye for art work, clever formatting, and logo design.

Your sign and your outdoor play area attract attention, and will silently recruit future children as yet unborn as their parents pass your program and find it appealing. You can extend this impact by having open houses and inviting the public. Your fund-raising events, such as bake sales, fairs, children's movies, guest speakers, musical entertainments, and the like, can also be designed to appeal to and entice parents that might want to use your service. In the same way you might develop a booth for the county fair, or a float for the local parade. Television and radio spots and newspaper features help. If you ask parents who enroll how they heard of your program, you will begin to evaluate what you are doing that reaches the most parents.

Waiting List Policies

Waiting lists are useful to the program as a pool from which to fill spaces without loss of time in recruitment of new children. They are also useful in order to document need for expanded services in your area to the media, and to policymakers in government. It would be extremely useful to do a little research on what happens to families when they are not able to get into the day care they are seeking. All these uses for waiting lists are using the needs of parents and their children for the purposes of the stability and growth of the day care services. Waiting lists, however, are seen as valuable by parents as well. Their existence implies that the programs will be fair in admitting children as new spaces open up, and will not accept another family on an unfair basis. It is important that their expectation of fairness be taken seriously.

As government broadens the number of people eligible for day care subsidy in the future, and as needs for day care increase, it will become increasingly important to have fair waiting list procedures. Even now, you need to be sure your policy on accepting families is fair to everybody. The Constitution requires such fairness, and your use of government subsidy that came from taxation will leave you vulnerable to lawsuits unless your records indicate that you accept people from the waiting list according to policy.

One criterion would be the time of application. Of two equally deserving families, it is fair to accept the one who applied first. Some centers have their own, other priorities, and would accept a family in a dire emergency ahead of a family that had been waiting for a long time. If so, this policy should be written down. For government subsidized "slots" a program may be required by the government to follow state priorities in accepting families from the waiting list. An example of such an order of priorities, different from one state to another, might be:

1. Cases of child abuse or neglect

2. Aid to Families with Dependent Children (A.F.D.C.) parents in work or training

3. Emergency family problems, children at risk of neglect or abuse

4. Parents who are employed, not welfare-related, but within income eligibility definitions

5. Other income eligible families

Massachusetts gives priority for continuity. That is, children already accepted have a right to continue, and pay higher fees even if higher priority categories are waiting. If your state does not have such a policy, you might be required to drop a child out of your program, or into a non-subsidized "slot."

When filling a space in demand by more than one person, priorities can

49

be your own, and they can also be the priorities of the state for certain "slots" they are buying from you. Even so, you will need to retain the right to balance groups by age and sex and in other ways. That kind of consideration will determine whether a "slot" has opened up, and for whom. You cannot fill a slot for a girl in your three-year-old group with a five-year-old boy; it is not that kind of a "slot."

As parents are placed on your waiting list, you should explain to them what the conditions are for deciding that a slot is available for a particular age and sex of child, and what the priorities for acceptance are among the families that are waiting for that kind of slot. You should also explain to them that you will automatically drop names off the waiting list after six months (if that is your policy), and that they should let you know then if they wish to be kept on the list. If you want to be extra fair, you might send postcards to those being dropped from the list about two weeks before it is time to cross off the names. You should not cut off the waiting list if parents wish to be placed on it, but you can explain that there is little or no chance of their getting in when the list reaches a certain length.

Setting Parent Fees

Fee setting is a complicated set of decisions. If you set the fees based on what parents can afford to pay, about 10% of their gross family income, or if you set fees based on the "going rate" in the community, you may not generate enough income to cover the costs of operating the kind of program you want. You might be forced to subsidize the program through underpaying your staff, accepting as a given the very low salaries in the field of day care. If you set your fees based on reasonable expected costs, they may come out considerably higher than the "going rate" and you may fail to attract many parents.

In the section on "break-even analysis" on page 54, you will find some further information and methods that will help in computing fees.

More and more, day care programs are trying to find ways to provide parents the opportunity to pay what they can afford of their day care with a sliding fee scale, and subsidizing the part that parents cannot pay. In a few communities, United Way supplements parents' fees on a sliding fee basis. In some states, the government pays the part of a sliding fee scale that parents cannot afford to pay. A few employers supplement what their employees can afford to pay through a voucher system.

There is also a tax credit for parents who pay for child day care. The following chart shows the dollar amounts of credits available at different income levels.

Parents should be informed by centers how to use the tax credit, and in particular how to get their withholding tax adjusted so that they have the money to pay for their child care on payday instead of having to wait until the end of the year. This handbook includes a handout for parents for this

| Adjusted Gross Income | Percentage | Maximum Credits | |
		One Child or Dependent	Two or More Children or Dependents
Up to $10,000	30%	$720	$1,440
10,001–12,000	29%	696	1,392
12,001–14,000	28%	672	1,344
14,001–16,000	27%	648	1,296
16,001–18,000	26%	624	1,248
18,001–20,000	25%	600	1,200
20,001–22,000	24%	576	1,152
22,001–24,000	23%	552	1,104
24,001–26,000	22%	528	1,056
26,001–28,000	21%	504	1,008
28,000 and over	20%	480	960

purpose. A statement should be given parents at income tax time of what they have spent in the day care program in the current tax year.

Parent fees, therefore, are already subsidized for 20–30% of what they pay. Sometimes government and employers or United Way will help with additional subsidy to bring the fees of day care within parents' ability to pay, on a sliding basis.

A sliding fee scale can be expressed by an amount which is greater or smaller in direct proportion to the income level of the parent. It is usually expressed in terms of dollars and cents. Another approach is to have a sliding percentage of income that parents have to pay that is a little higher as income rises.

A sliding fee is based on the concept of a full fee charged at the top for parents who can afford it, with a graduated scale below that requires parents to pay less and less at lower and lower income levels, and standardized in tables for families with different numbers of children.

Some programs have tried to set the top, or full fee, higher than the cost of the service, in an effort to have the high-income parents subsidize the lower-income parents. That policy has seldom worked, since the full cost of day care is so great that very few parents would willingly pay still more to help out families with less ability to pay. A "Robin Hood" fee schedule is not usually acceptable to parents.

Parents' Questions About the Child Care Tax Credit

A Handout Factsheet

If you spend money on child care you can get between 20% and 30% of what you spent, depending on your income, taken out of the tax bill you owe the federal government at income tax time. There are limits to $2400 for an only child or $4800 for more than one child that can be claimed.

WHO CAN GET THE TAX CREDIT?
You can qualify if you:

work, part-time or full-time, for pay, or are searching for employment

do not earn less than you pay for child care (either spouse)

have one or more children under age 15 for whom you are entitled to a personal exemption

are a single person or have a spouse who also works or is a full-time student, 5 months of the year, or is disabled

you are withholding Social Security taxes, or if they work for another organization that provides child care; and not if they are your dependents.

WHAT IF MY CHILD CARE IS SUBSIDIZED?
If the government or somebody else pays part of your child care, you are not spending money on that, and therefore cannot claim a credit for your costs. But if you pay anything, you can claim that part of the care that you have to pay for, since it is an expense to you.

WILL THE CREDIT APPLY TO ALL MY TAXES?
No. The credit only applies to your federal personal income tax. Some states have a deduction or credit for your state personal income tax, but not all.

DO I HAVE TO WAIT UNTIL THE END OF THE YEAR TO GET THE CREDIT?
No. The credit can increase your paycheck, to make it possible for you to have money to spend on your child care, IF you claim it when you fill

WHAT CHILD CARE EXPENSES CAN BE COUNTED?

Everything you have to spend on child care so you can work counts, except:

anything above $2400 for an only child and $4800 for all your children

costs of transportation from home to care

child care expenses that are greater than what you earn, if you are single, or greater than what the lowest paid spouse earns in a married couple.

WHAT PERCENT OF MY EXPENSES MAY I SUBTRACT FROM MY TAX?

If your income is under $10,000 your credit is 30%. For every $2000 you earn above $10,000 deduct 1% from the credit, unless your income is above $28,000 at which point the credit remains 20%.

WHAT TYPE OF CHILD CARE COUNTS?

Payments you make to day care centers, nursery schools, family day care providers, and babysitters in your home can all be claimed.

CAN I PAY MY RELATIVES?

Not unless they are your employees for whom

HOW DO I CLAIM THE CREDIT?

You may use either the long form (1040) or the short form (1040A). Whichever form you use, you must attach to it the Form for Credit for Child and Dependent Care Expense (2441). On it you must itemize your child care expenses. You will need to have receipts for these expenses in your files.

HOW DO I GET MY PAYCHECK INCREASED?

Fill out a new W-4 form at your place of employment; with only one employer if you have more than one job. On it, list what you pay per week for child care; multiply by the number of weeks you will use the child care. This annual expected cost can then be multiplied by the percent credit to which you are entitled, up to the limits. Use this amount to determine from the table on the reverse side of the form the number of allowances you should claim. This number will usually be *more than the number of dependents*. Your federal tax withheld will be reduced by this amount, and your next paycheck will be bigger. But if you overestimated, you'll have to pay the government later, so be careful.

Even a fee scale based on real costs as the top fee causes some misunderstanding among parents in some programs, who seem to feel that they are being penalized when they pay the higher fees. Because of this potential for misunderstanding, some programs offer a sliding scholarship aid program instead of a sliding fee. The result is exactly the same, but the parents better understand that they are being subsidized, and they accept better the fact that the subsidy is less for higher-income parents.

Collecting the Fees

Most day care programs, whether for-profit or not-for-profit, end up at some time or other providing a service for parents who simply cannot pay for it. There are many heartrending cases that directors just cannot turn away, at least for awhile. On the other hand, the program itself will fail, and all the other families will lose their valuable service, if the fees the program depends on are not collected. All day care administrators face this dilemma.

The successful administrators whose programs survive report that they are firm, consistent, and quick to follow-up in their fee collection processes. The less successful administrators are those whose commitment to humanity has led them to establish relaxed procedures that let a parent get too far in debt before they try to catch up with the situation. It seems clear that, from the perspective of parents as well as day care providers, clear policies with quick follow-up are important.

Fee collecting is also so time-consuming that it adds considerably to administrative costs unless serious attention is given to streamlining the procedures themselves. If parents are permitted to pay at any time of the week, time is required from the program staff that adds up. If parents all pay on the same day, one staff person can handle the whole procedure in one part of the day, and get the money to the bank where it will be safe, with a minimum of wasted effort. It is therefore desirable to ask parents who pay by check through the mail to get their payments in the same week, and those who pay in person and in cash to do it only on one day each week set aside for the purpose. For the cash payments, you should use a numbered receipt book with carbon copies, which will enable you to have a record on file as a cross check for your attendance and fee record. Your deposit slip for the bank should list the names of those paying, and this can be photocopied for your files.

Break-Even Analysis

A break-even analysis is a way of determining how to price your service. Alternatively, in a situation where a program has a fixed fee already, such as a set reimbursement from the state, a break-even analysis enables you to determine how many children you have to have before you will break even, if you ever do.

To break even is to reach the point where income and expenditures exactly balance. Break-even analysis is especially useful when a new program is starting up. It tells you at what number of children or at what fees you will break even, which you will need to know in order to determine how long you must operate at a loss, and how much cash reserve you will need before you turn the break-even corner. When you add on new program components, such as infant care, or after-school care, to an existing service, break-even analysis again becomes useful.

If your program's size and fees remain fairly stable from year to year, a break-even analysis is useful only if you want to rethink the numbers of children or the fees charged. This might happen if the program is not doing well, or if it loses a stable source of outside funds.

There are two ways of pinpointing the break-even points. One is a formula calculation, and the other is a graphic presentation. Both methods depend on an analysis of fixed costs and variable costs. For day care it is useful to add another concept of semi-variable costs.

Fixed costs are those costs that you will have no matter how many children you have in your program. These costs are the same; they do not vary by numbers of children. They include your overhead, rent, office salaries of the executive, and the costs of interest and depreciation.

Variable costs are those costs directly associated with the number of children you have, and they include the costs of food and supplies. For every child you add, you directly add a cost in this category.

Staff costs in day care are variable, because you need more staff if you add more children. But they do not vary directly with the number of children. Instead they vary with clumps of children. You might have two staff members and eleven children, for example, and you could add a twelfth child, and then another and another, without changing the number of staff, until you reach the point where one more child makes the group too large. At that point, you would need another staff person, after which time you could again add more children without adding staff. Because of the nature of day care, it is helpful to consider staff costs to be semi-variable; that is they vary in steps, as groups of children are added, rather than directly, as you add child by child to the program.

The formula for break-even is simple:

$$R = F + V + S$$

where R = Revenues
              F = Fixed Costs
              V = Variable Costs
   and S = Semi-variable Costs.

For day care, the left side of the equation needs to be made a little more complex. In the case of a day care program dependent on fees from parents and/or the government, R can be considered NT.

where N = Number of Children
and T = Full Per-Child Tuition or Fee.

If you have analyzed your budget into fixed, variable, and semi-variable costs, you can then put numbers into the equation. For example:

NT = $30,000 (Fixed Costs) + $20,000 (Variable Costs) + $80,000 (Semi-variable)

If your licensed capacity is 50 children, then the number of children could be a given, and your problem becomes 50T = $130,000, and therefore your fee must be $2,600 per year, with a little more added for utilization factor.

However, if you cannot charge $2,600 a year, either because the parents cannot afford it or the state will not pay it, then you have a different problem.

In this case, you might have to decide what fee you can set, and then work out the other variables. For example, if you decide you can charge $35 per week (collecting $1,820 in 52 weeks), you could set up your equation in one of three ways.

(1)   N × $1,820 = $130,000. This tells you that you need 72 children to break even. However, your licensed capacity may be less than 72, and the variable and semi-variable costs that you projected may not cover the staff you need for that many children.

(2)   If your licensed capacity is 50, you would have to set up your equation this way:

$1,820 × 50 = $30,000 + V + S
$91,000 = $30,000 + X

X or the combination of variable and semi-variable costs is $61,000. You will have to reduce some of these costs from your budgeted $100,000.

(3)   If you are not able to reduce any of your costs, you will have to add another source of funds as an item on the left side of the equation.

$91,000 + X = $130,000.

X, your fund-raising amount, is $39,000, and would have to be raised every year.

Break-Even Chart

A break-even chart is a quick and useful way of presenting this break-even information graphically. You may prepare several such charts, showing different cases you want to compare, for presentation to the board or a funding source. A break-even chart looks like the one on the following page.

56

The variable costs have been divided between variable and semi-variable costs, for day care purposes. Variable costs vary directly with every change in the number of children; semi-variable costs vary only after a certain number of children have been added. For example, you will need one peanut butter sandwich for one child, five for five children, twenty for twenty children, etc. This is a variable cost. You will need one staff person for one child, one for four children, two for eight children, (or whatever the number is where you think you would need to add another staff person), two for eleven children, and so on until you will reach the number of children you need for a third staff person. This is a semi-variable cost.

If you plot just variable costs on a graph, they would start at the cost for one child and rise on a slant as number of children increased. If you plot just semi-variable costs on another graph, they would start at the cost for one child and continue flat until the point where you need to add another staff person, then they would jump straight up to a higher level, where they would continue straight again until the next staff increase is indicated. The effect would be a staircase profile. If you plot your fixed costs on a graph, they would start at a certain level well above zero, and continue at that level in a straight line.

The break-even chart presents these three graphs on top of one another as a picture of total costs. Fixed costs are portrayed across the bottom section of the graph. They are the same level, regardless of number of children. On top of these fixed costs, and added to them, is a middle area of costs, the variable costs, that vary exactly with the number of children. Since these costs are placed on top of the fixed costs, the top line represents the sum of fixed and variable costs.

The top section of the graph represents placing the semi-variable costs on top of all the other costs. The area between the top of the slant line (fixed and variable costs) and the top line is the semi-variable cost area. The top line represents the total cost of the program, since these semi-variable costs have been added on at the top of all the other costs.

The break-even points are circled, where the rising income line crosses the top line representing total costs. There are likely to be two or more break-even points, with points between them where the program does not break even. Between these points, the program would lose money.

How To Do A Break-Even Chart

1. On a sheet of graph paper, develop a horizontal axis across the bottom, and a vertical axis along the side. The vertical axis, representing dollars, starts at 0 and rises by $1,000s along the side of your graph. The horizontal axis, along the bottom, represents numbers of children, starting at 0 and increasing up to the maximum licensed capacity of your center or family day care system.

BREAK-EVEN CHART

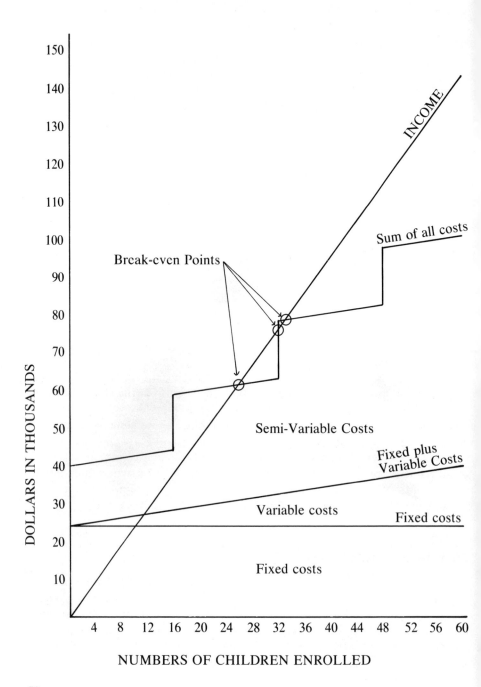

150
140
130
120
110
100
90
80
70
60
50
40
30
20
10

INCOME

Sum of all costs

Break-even Points

Semi-Variable Costs

Fixed plus
Variable Costs

Variable costs

Fixed costs

Fixed costs

DOLLARS IN THOUSANDS

4   8   12   16   20   24   28   32   36   40   44   48   52   56   60

NUMBERS OF CHILDREN ENROLLED

2. *Fixed Costs*. Calculate all those costs that you will incur regardless of the numbers of children enrolled. You should be aware that if you are not able to reach a break-even point with these fixed costs, you will probably have to go back and rethink these fixed costs, but they represent your best thinking for this first graphic presentation.

3. *Variable Costs*. These costs will be tied directly to your enrollment. As numbers of children are added, costs are added in direct proportion. Examples are food and curriculum supplies. You can plot these costs on another graph and overlay or place them on top of the first graph. Or you can plot them on your graph as if the level of fixed costs were the starting point or zero level for the variable costs at the left. The top line of this middle section will be the sum of your fixed plus variable costs.

4. *Semi-variable Costs*. Staff costs in direct care of children do not increase evenly as each child is added. Staff costs will remain constant until they reach the point (in numbers of children) at which you need to add more staff, and then jump to a new flat level as each new teacher is added, like stairs. You can plot these costs on another graph, and overlay or paste it on top of the break-even chart, but you would have to put it on an angle, since the top of your cost level for fixed and variable costs is a slanted line. Or you can calculate each step as total costs, and start your top line by plotting the point where the first staff costs would be included in the overall budget, then placing the next point and the next. Once you have all these points identified, you can connect them with a ruler, by making the line parallel the fixed and variable line until it is directly below your plotted point, then rise straight up to the point, then parallel the fixed and variable line until directly below the next point, and so on. This top line looks like a slanted staircase, since it represents total costs with the sudden rises that are part of semi-variable costs represented as the risers of the stairs, and the slanted variable costs represented as the steps themselves.

5. *Plot your income line*. This will be a straight line that can be drawn with a ruler, since income will increase directly with each child added, according to the fee charged. If your annual fee is $1,500, for example, the income would increase by $3,000 for every two children. The point at which this rising income line intersects with the top line, or total costs line, is the break-even point. Until the center enrolls the number of children shown, it will not break even—it will lose money. It is also common to lose the break-even capability above that exact point, and then to hit another break-even point later, indicating that under certain conditions after you have reached the break-even point you may again lose money unless you are careful.

It is useful, for decision purposes, to prepare several charts to compare several situations. You may, if you are adding an infant group to a program and want to compare different fee policies, prepare two or three charts at different fees. You might prepare charts showing the effect of different levels of fixed costs. The break-even analysis is useful as an internal decision-making tool for boards. For sources of funds, it can be a good tool to indicate that you have done your homework and know exactly how long you need working capital and when that period will come to an end when the program turns the break-even corner, and reaches stability.

4. THE EXPENDITURE SIDE OF THE BUDGET

This handbook has presented a start-up budget, and an annual operating budget to assist in understanding expenditures, and the ways in which they must be balanced by income. This type of budget is the starting point for understanding expenditures.

In addition to the line-item budget, with its face sheet and detailed breakdowns of information, there are a number of other useful ways of organizing budget information for analyzing expenditures in relation to income. These are:

a program budget

functional budget analysis

cash flow

The Program Budget

If you run a single day care center, then your line item budget is a program budget, because you are running one program. If you decide to add another center in another location, or to add a family day care satellite system or an infant program, you will understand what is happening in your various programs better if you keep your numbers separated on paper, through program budgeting. This is not difficult to do.

Most of the costs of each program, such as the salaries of staff who work only in one program, will clearly belong in the program's budget. There will be a few costs shared across programs. For example, there might be a social worker working 50% of the time in each of two programs. Or the director's cost might be allocated 75% at the day care center and 25% in the smaller family day care program (or vice versa). Costs of office supplies would be spread in the same way as would be a bookkeeper or secretary who worked for both programs.

Functional Budgeting

Functional budgeting becomes useful when it is important to compare the costs of different programs. This becomes important when public funds are involved, as in setting rates of reimbursement for Title XX. You will notice that on page 17 there is information comparing costs for different functions across twenty centers. Using a standardized functional budget system, policymakers can compare costs of different programs, or different types of programs, accurately.

For the manager of several programs, functional budgeting permits you to compare the costs of your different functions to see whether one program has higher costs than another for the same function. You might find that one program has higher administrative costs than you want, or that transportation costs more in relation to the overall budget than is feasible. You might try to develop programs, such as drop-in care, that have the potential of helping to pay for some of your other programs, and functional budgeting will help you to analyze whether this is happening.

A great deal of research over the last decade has gone into developing functional budgeting processes for day care. Some states base their reimbursement rate for Title XX day care contracts on cost data developed through functional budget analysis.

The standard functions which have been developed for cost analysis in day care are:

> care and teaching
> administration
> feeding
> health services
> transportation
> occupancy
> parent services
> staff development and special functions

These functions are not the same as the items in the line item budget presented on page 21. You will note that there is no line item for supplies, for example, since supplies will be used within the different *functions* of the day care program, some for care and teaching, some for administration, some for feeding, some for health. The personnel section is missing here, also, since the personnel costs will be attributed to the functions they perform. Some

THIS IS A SAMPLE PROGRAM BUDGET FOR A PROGRAM OPERATING A CENTER, SATELLITE HOME PROGRAM, AND INFANT PROGRAM

Model Day Care Program, Annual Budget July 1, _____

Face Sheet	Center Program	Family Day Care Program	Infant Program
Personnel			
Director			
Administrative staff			
Classroom staff			
Social Service staff			
Domestic/Maintenance			
Health Personnel			
Cook			
Fringe Benefits			
Contract Service and Consultants			
Supplies			
Occupancy			
Furniture, Equipment, and Vehicles			
Conferences, Special Events			
Other Expenses			
TOTALS			

Use back-up sheets as in line item budget

THIS IS A WORKSHEET FORMAT FOR CALCULATING PAYROLL COSTS FOR FUNCTIONAL

BUDGETING

Gross pay and Employer's share of Fringe Benefits
(Some figures inserted as examples)

Day Care Program,
July 1, 1982–July 1, 1983

Name and Position	Gross Pay and Fringe	Admin.	Food	Child Care & Teaching	Health	Transp.	Occupancy	Parent Services	Special Functions
Jane Jones Director	14,375	11,300							3,075
Anne Fairchild Cook	5,000	5,000							
Anna Smith Social Worker	9,050							9,050	
Adam Friendly Driver-Janitor	6,100					3,050	3,050		
Daniel Boone Classroom Teacher	8,000			8,000					
Etc.									
TOTALS									

THIS IS A WORKSHEET FORMAT FOR CALCULATING SUPPLIES COSTS FOR FUNCTIONAL BUDGETING

Accounting can keep data in a form similar to this to permit cost analysis by function.

SUPPLIES — Day Care Program; July 1, 1982 – July 1, 1983

	Date	Items	1 Admin.	2 Food	3 Child Care #Teaching	4 Health	5 Transp.	6 Occupancy	7 Parent Services	8 Special Functions
1	Jul 1	Best Foods		300						
2	3	Smiley Toys			80					
3	3	Diapers			20					
4	5	Envelopes	15							
5	7	Gasoline					15			
6	8	Rental Film								4
7	8	Conference								
8	10	Paper Cups		10						45
9	11	Oil						300		
10	14	Floor Cleaner						10		
11										
12		TOTALS	15	310	100		15	310		49
13										

staff salaries will be budgeted entirely in one function, such as those of classroom teachers who do nothing else. Some will be spread over several functions, such as a director who counsels parents, trains staff, and substitutes in the classroom to any significant extent. In preparing a functional budget, it is not useful to nitpick over very minor matters, such as adding up ten minutes of sweeping done by a classroom teacher under occupancy.

The function of feeding will consist of all the costs for food, paper cups, and other supplies, plus the time spent by the cook in preparing the food. The items for payroll, supplies, and equipment will have to be analyzed and an estimated amount allocated to each function.

In order to make these calculations that allocate costs to function, the program's bookkeeping system will have to differentiate items of supplies and equipment by function. Functional cost accounting for supplies and equipment is easier to do if the program's chart of accounts, used in bookkeeping, matches the functional categories. Supplies and equipment are entered into the books with numbers that identify their function, so that costs by function can later be compiled. An example of such a chart of accounts is given in the Appendix. Payroll analysis is done either by research-like time sheets if more information on staff time is needed, or is estimated by percentages based on the director's knowledge of how staff are paid to spend their time.

Worksheets are used which list supplies and equipment, and then assign their costs to the correct column of functions spread out horizontally on a page. The same type of analysis is done for payroll.

5. CASH FLOW ANALYSIS

A cash flow analysis is the most critical planning tool for a new day care program, for one which is growing or adding different programs, or for one which extends or is extended very much credit.

It is possible in day care to be in a position of balanced books, where income is greater than expenditure, and everything looks rosy on paper, but at the same time find that there is no money in the bank and the payroll cannot be met next Tuesday.

It is important for anyone managing a day care program to understand that this can happen, and how it can happen. If there were no such thing as credit—if every parent paid every day for their day care, if teachers were paid every day, and all purchases made in cash—there could not be a situation when the cash position of a day care program would be disastrous while assets and liabilities balance favorably. Yet, because of the differences in the time at which expenditures are made or income comes in, it is not uncommon for the line item budget to show a strong surplus, while at the same time the center cannot pay its bills and creditors are bringing suit. The money may be flowing out of the organization much more rapidly than it is flowing in, if the inflow is mostly credit and the outflow is mostly cash. Ironically, this kind of disaster is most likely to affect a successful, growing program in high demand. Many a small organization has been wiped out by its growth and success, if cash flow planning was neglected.

Cash flow deals only with actual cash transactions, regardless of who owes money to the center, or obligations of the center to pay others. It does not tell you what your assets and liabilities are if you have to close your doors. You do not want to close your doors. You want to know what your cash position is at any given time, and what it will be in the future. An analysis of your cash flow will give you this needed information.

To do a cash flow budget, list every item in which money changes hands at the time that happens. Loan repayments, including interest, are included in a cash flow, since money changes hands. Depreciation, on the other hand, is not, since it is not a cash expense. List the payments from the Welfare Department in the month it comes in, not the month the obligation was incurred.

To analyze cash flow, you will first determine what your fixed costs are. For purposes of cash flow, fixed costs are those costs that would have to be met regardless of the numbers of children at the center—in other words, regardless of how much income is coming in.

Remember the analysis for purposes of break-even analysis where staff costs were generally considered to be semi-variable because they varied with groups of children. There you were analyzing a projected number of staff, for planning purposes, in order to determine what decisions to make. For purposes of cash flow, you are not looking at hypothetical, but real staff in some cases, and it becomes an issue whether you are going to regard these costs as fixed, in the sense that you have to pay them on the next payday, or whether they are semi-variable.

Because of your concern for continuity in day care, it is possible that you are going to staff up for your expected number of children, and feel an obligation to retain your staff through minor fluctuations of cash flow. You will know better than to staff for the whole year at the staffing needed only for peak periods, such as late September, because you will know that enrollment is going to fall off in other months. As you staff your program, you will anticipate staffing patterns across the year, rather than at peak periods.

FORMAT FOR CASH FLOW ANALYSIS

October, one month

A. *October Cash In* (Here you will list all the money that came in during October, early, late, or on time, and you will not list any money you are owed.)

Parent fees paid this month (regardless if in advance or arrears)   _____

USDA for August   _____

Other income during October   _____

    A.   TOTAL CASH IN FOR OCTOBER   _____

B. *October Cash Out* (All the money you actually spent, not unpaid bills)
List all variable cash expenditures:

Heat   _____

Supplies   _____

Advertising   _____

Transportation   _____

Continue listing all other   _____

    _____

    _____

Fixed Cash Out (an amount that you have figured out, the same every month, that is the least you have to pay out monthly)   _____

    B.   TOTAL CASH OUT   _____
    (all variable cash out added to fixed cash out)

C. *Cash Flow* (the difference between A, Total   _____
Cash In, and B, Total Cash Out. B is subtracted
from A. If A is less than B, the number will be a
negative number, entered in parentheses.)

D. *Cumulative Cash Flow.* Add this month's cash   _____
flow to last month's cumulative cash flow. If you did
not do a cash flow in previous months, add it this month
to the cash you had on hand on September 31, and then
in next month's cash flow, use the October cumulative
cash flow to add here.

Having made your decisions about the core staff you need, you are probably going to regard your obligation to that staff as fixed, even if your enrollment falls off slightly differently than anticipated. It is important in a cash flow analysis to think through very carefully what staff you are going to consider to be fixed costs, even in the face of a dangerous financial situation, what staff you think could be reduced if income reduces, and what disasters might cause you to rethink these decisions.

A monthly cash flow analysis follows this general form:

First, figure out what all the fixed costs are—the ones that you are obligated to pay every single month. This includes your rent and other related costs, your core staff, and food for the children. This adds up to a single number. Day care directors facing financial crises have this number etched indelibly on their brains. All day care directors should have a working familiarity with such a number, especially if the organization operates marginally close to its break-even point.

In the example which follows, the director has determined that almost all costs are considered fixed. Salaries, food, electricity, and telephone are included in fixed costs. The center pays no rent, so that is not a cost. On ledger paper, about three-fourths of the way down the page, the director has figured the fixed costs to be $7,709.62, and has drawn a little box around this figure. This is going to be the amount of money which that director will have to come up with every month, come what may. If the center is operating close to the brink of financial disaster, that amount becomes an important one for the director to carry around in his or her head. It becomes a calculation which goes on constantly in the mind. The closer the danger becomes of not being able to meet the obligation, the more indelibly the figure is etched into the director's brain.

Under "fixed costs" you will find the figure $7,709.62 appearing in each monthly column in the example.

The example is a *cash flow projection,* rather than a simple monthly analysis as explained on the previous page. It is a best guess estimate of what the future will hold in the twelve-month period the director wants to project. Studying the example may help you to understand how and why to do cash flow projections.

In the September column, at the far left, at the top of the page, the director has added together all the cash which actually comes in, in September—not what is owed. Here the total cash receipts will be $9,950 in September.

Each month, the total cash disbursed is going to consist of all the variable costs, listed one by one as expected, plus that figure of $7,709.62 which is the fixed costs.

The net cash flow is the difference between the cash coming in (receipts) and the cash going out (disbursements). In September, continuing to read down the column in the example, the net cash flow is $2,140.38. There is no cumulative cash flow, since the director did not make a cash flow analysis in August.

In October, the director is predicting what will happen, using the same format, and gets a net cash flow of $1,165.38. This net cash flow is then added to the cash flow figure from the preceding month of September, to get October's cumulative cash flow. It is this figure, $3,305.76, which is the key line to look at in the cash flow projections for the remaining months.

You will notice in the example that in January and February, there is a temporary cash flow problem, and a more serious one in June and July, which necessitates a bank loan because the center does not have the working capital to cover it.

Across the bottom of the page, the director is adding the receipts for the month to the cash on hand, subtracting the cash disbursements, and arriving at an actual cash balance which takes into account the fact that there was $800 on hand when the analysis began in September.

A cash flow analysis is useful in several ways. First, for the program operating close to the margin, or engaging in a multitude of credit transactions, it tells you what the actual cash position is, and it accustoms you to thinking about your fixed cash costs and how you are going to meet them each month with cash.

A projection of cash flow over a twelve-month period enables you to see what the maximum cash deficit you might have over the course of a year would probably be, to operate your program. In the example, the maximum cash flow shortage is $4,517.62. If the center had that amount of money in the bank, as a cushion against cash flow problems, there could never be a time when the cash flowing out depleted the cash needed to meet obligations. This figure is the *working capital* you need to operate in the black. Knowing what it is, you may be able to get a commitment from your board for fund raising to assure that amount of cash on hand, or you may be able to get a bank to loan you the money.

If you are part of a larger organization, then that larger organization has probably been absorbing your cash flow temporary shortages. A cash flow analysis gives you information about your operation which you were not aware of, because the traditional balance sheets did not give it to you, and because you were protected by the useful financial buffer provided by the larger organization. It may help you in understanding your financial position in the other organization; it may also help the other organization to understand situations where you create temporary financial strains.

Community Day Care
CASH FLOW

		Sept	Oct	Nov	Dec	Jan
1	Cash Receipts					
2	Parent fees	4450	3560	3360	4025	317
3	Title XX	5000	5200	6125	5140	494
4	USDA	500	500	556 25	392	37
5	Total Receipts	9950	9260	10041 25	9557	849
6						
7						
8	Cash Disbursed					
9	Heat	100	150	200	200	20
10	Supplies	—	—	718 62	—	—
11	Advertising	—	10	—	300	—
12	Transportation	—	—	—	20	1
13	Ed. materials	—	—	—	—	
14	Staff devel.	—	225	—	—	
15	Insurance	—	—	—	—	
16	Legal, audit fees	—	—	—	—	75
17	Total variable	100	385	918 62	520	96
18	Fixed cash disbursed *	7709 62	7709 62	7709 62	7709 62	770
19	Interest on loans	—	—	—	—	—
20	Total Disbursed	7809 62	8094 62	8628 24	8229 62	866
21						
22						
23	Net Cash Flow	2140 38	1165 38	1413 01	1327 38	(17
24	Cumulative Cash Flow	2140 38	3305 76	4718 77	6046 15	586
25						
26						
27	*	Fixed Cash Disbursements:				
28		Salaries		6047 50		
29		Fringe		907 12		
30		Elec. & Tel.		100		
31		Food		655		
32		Total		7709 62		
33						
34						
35						
36	Cash on Hand at start of month	800	2940 38	4105 76	5518 77	6846
37	Receipts	9950	9260	10041 25	9557	8490
38	Total balance	10750	12200 38	14147 01	15075 77	15336
39	Less cash disbursements	7809 62	8094 62	8628 24	8229 62	8669
40	Total New Balance	2940 38	4105 76	5518 77	6846 15	6666

	Feb	Mar	Apr	May	June	July	Aug	Total	
1									
2	3080	3360	3360	4450	3260	3260	3060	42400	
3	3975	5075	4660	4900	—	—	16465	61480	
4	369	353	354	40475	342	330	360	4836	
5	7424	8788	8374	975475	3602	3590	19885	108716	
6									
7									
8									
9	200	200	150	100	—	—	—	1500	
10	71862	—	—	71863	—	—	171863	387450	
11	—	—	—	—	400	—	300	1010	
12	10	—	—	10	10	15	15	90	
13	—	—	—	—	—	—	150	150	
14	—	225	—	—	—	—	50	500	
15	—	—	—	—	—	—	100	100	
16	—	—	—	—	—	—	—	750	
17	92862	425	150	82863	410	15	233363	797450	
18	770962	770962	770962	770962	770962	770962	770962	9251544	
19	—	—	—	—	—	—	—	—	
20	863824	813462	785962	853825	811962	772462	1004325	9388994	
21									
22									
23	(121424)	65538	51438	121650	(451762)	(413462)	984175		
24	465229	530567	582005	703655	251893	(161569)	822606		
25									
26									
27									
28									
29									
30									
31									
32									
33									
34									
35									
36	666653	545229	610567	662005	783655	331893	(81569)		
37	7424	8788	8374	975475	3602	3590	19885		
38	1409053	1424029	1447967	1637480	1143855	690893	1906931		
39	863824	813462	785962	853825	811962	772462	1004325		
40	545229	610567	662005	783655	331893	(81569)	902606		

6. Accrual Accounting and Budgeting

Accrual accounting and budgeting is the opposite of cash flow budgeting. Accrual means spreading out uneven lumps of expenditures evenly across the months of the year. That is very useful in preventing you from mistaking a favorable cash position at a particular time as a signal to spend, when you have a need to reserve the money for future obligations. It is less useful, however, in short-term crises. The larger the organization, the less likely it is that cash flow analysis will be a central tool for decision-making, but both accrual analysis and cash flow analysis have their important uses in day care organizations of all types.

7. Deviation Analysis, Income Statements, and Balance Sheets

The line item budget, presented as this handbook began, is in its one-page form what is called an income statement, or a statement of income and expense, or a profit and loss statement. When these statements are cast into the future, they are called projections, or *pro forma* statements. The form is standardized to permit easy comparison and analysis. It must always be dated.

Reports can be prepared in this form of what has been spent, and compared with what was planned to be spent. At least quarterly, it is important to compare actual spending with planned spending, to identify any deviations from the plan. You need to detect deviations before they turn into cumulative disasters.

Deviation analysis can be presented on paper using the standard form of an income statement, or it can be done with a functional budget statement or a cash flow budget.

The following format combines an income statement with deviation analysis as a management tool. You should fill out this form yourself or work with your accountant to get it done in the form that is most useful to you. If you are using a cash flow as a monthly budget tool, you could take your cash flow budget and add to it the extra columns, just as the following sample does for the income statement. The monthly cash flow budget would be column B. Column A would tell you what you had actually spent that month. Column C would tell you the difference between what you spent and what you planned to spend. Column D would give you the percent by which you deviated from your budget plan.

The example given follows the format of an Annual Income Statement. The first column, on the final month of the year, is a statement which you should prepare each year as part of your Annual Report. In the example, which would be prepared quarterly, the first column is the amount spent at this point in the year; the second column is the amount budgeted to this point in the year; and the last columns give the dollar and percent deviations. This type of deviation analysis can follow the form of functional budgets as well as of income and expenditures, as shown, or cash flow.

After the form on the following page, you will find a similar one, for a monthly deviation analysis.

Balance Sheets

Balance sheets are designed to show how the assets, liabilities, and net worth of an organization balance out at a given point in time. A standard form is used so that comparisons can be made. Unlike income and expense statements, it does not present a moving picture of the activities of the organization. Instead, it is like a still photograph of the organization, capturing its financial picture.

You will not need a balance sheet more than annually, unless you have to prepare one for a bank loan or a funding source. It is likely that an accountant will prepare the balance sheet for you. However, you should understand the form and how to read it.

There are many books on the subject of analyzing a balance sheet; for example, the free publication, *How to Read A Financial Report,* from Merrill, Lynch, Pierce, Fenner, and Smith.

Current Assets are the money you have, and everything which you could fairly readily turn into cash. That includes bills you expect to be paid, deposits you can get back, and the like. *Fixed assets* are those assets you have which would be harder to turn into cash, and they include buildings and land and the improvements you have made in them, major equipment, and depreciation.

Current Liabilities are those debts you have which you must pay in the short run. *Long-term liabilities* are debts you must ultimately pay, including long-term loans, the investment which the owner has made, and the like.

THIS IS A BUDGET DEVIATION ANALYSIS
INCOME AND EXPENDITURES

Year to date _____

	A Year to Date	B Budget to Date	C Deviation B − A	D % Deviation $\frac{C}{B} \times 100$
REVENUE				
Tuition				
Donations				
Government				
Foundation				
Other				
Total revenues				
EXPENSES				
Salaries				
Payroll Tax				
Repairs and Maintenance				
Consultants				
Mortgage Interest or Rent				
Depreciation				
Licenses and Fees				
Insurance				
Telephone				
Utilities				
Supplies				
Equipment				
Food				
Travel				
Miscellaneous				
Total expenses				
NET INCOME				
Tax expense if any				
Net profit after taxes (for-profit)				

CALCULATIONS: A. *ADD* current month actual expenses to last month's year to date analysis.
B. *ADD* current month budget to last month's year to date analysis.

This is a Budget Deviation Analysis
Income and Expenditures

Month _____

	A Actual for Month	B Budget for Month	C Deviation B − A	D % Deviation $\dfrac{C}{B} \times 100$
REVENUE				
Tuition				
Donations				
Government				
Foundation				
Other				
Total revenues				
EXPENSES				
Salaries				
Payroll Tax				
Repairs and Maintenance				
Consultants				
Mortgage Interest or Rent				
Depreciation				
Licenses and Fees				
Insurance				
Telephone				
Utilities				
Supplies				
Equipment				
Food				
Travel				
Miscellaneous				
Total expenses				
NET INCOME				
Tax expense, if any				
Net Profit after taxes (for-profit)				

BALANCE SHEET

_____(DATE)
AUDITED/NOT AUDITED

ASSETS

Current Assets:
  Cash _____
  Accounts receivable _____
  Utility deposits _____
    Total current assets _____

Fixed Assets
  Land _____
  Building _____
  Lease improvements _____
  Major equipment _____
    Total fixed assets _____
    Minus: accumulated
      depreciation _____
    Net fixed assets _____

TOTAL ASSETS _____

LIABILITIES & NET WORTH

Current Liabilities:
  Taxes payable, federal,
  state, FICA _____
  Health insurance, life
  and accident insurance _____
  Retirement _____
  Accounts payable _____
    Total current liabilities _____

Long-Term Liabilities
  Loans payable _____
  Mortgage _____
    Total long-term liabilities _____

Net Worth
  Owner's contributed equity _____
  Retained earnings _____
    Total _____

TOTAL LIABILITIES & NET WORTH _____

Two common ways of reading a balance sheet are to look at the current ratio, and to try the acid test.

Current ratio: Divide the current assets by the current liabilities. Business analysts like to see a rule of thumb of 2 to 1. However, for a not-for-profit day care center it is no cause for alarm if the ratio is 1 to 1, or a little better.

Acid test is calculated by dividing the most liquid assets, cash, securities, and accounts receivable by current liabilities. The most liquid assets are those you can immediately realize, and do not include utility deposits or some accounts receivable. Here the rule of thumb in business is 1.0, but in a not-for-profit day care center this may not be realistic.

8. COMBINING SOME OF THESE CONCEPTS

In the preceding sections, a number of different tools for analysis and management have been presented and explained. When you become familiar with these tools, you will know which are most useful to you in your situation. You will probably work out your own form which you use to compile the information you need to manage, regardless of the forms required of you for other purposes, such as reporting to your funding source, or to the Internal Revenue Service. The following are forms which several directors have developed for their use in management.

(A) The first form is a monthly analysis of expenditures and income that one director likes to spend two hours a month on. Her first three columns are similar to a cash flow budget, with deviation analysis. This tells the director where she stands with the finances at her center that month. She may find she has a lot of money in one line item, or be overspent in another. This is useful information, but the director likes to have a little more information about why this is so. Column 4 records what is owed to the center and what the center owes, which may help to explain why there is or is not cash in a particular budget item. This form therefore adds to cash flow information some further analysis of credit to help to explain the finances. The remainder of the columns compare this month's income and expenses with the budget for the year.

(A)   One director's monthly analysis, combining cash flow with credit analysis (column 4), and comparing income and expense with budget.

MONTHLY FINANCIAL STATEMENT

MONTH OF: ———————

	Monthly Actual	Monthly Projected	Actual vs. Projected
	1.	2.	3.
INCOME			
Private Income			
Welfare Contract			
Government Food Subsidy			
Private Community			
TOTAL INCOME			
EXPENSES			
Salaries			
Substitutes			
Work-Study			
Professional Fees: (Audit, Bank)			
Supplies			
Classrooms			
Office			
(Photocopies, Postage, etc.)			
Telephone			
Occupancy			
Rent			
Insurance			
Utilities			
Maintenance			
Food			
Consumables			
Unclassified			
TOTAL EXPENSE			
BUDGET JUSTIFICATION			

Payables & Receivables	YTD Actual	YTD Projected	Actual & Projected YTD Difference	Actual YTD plus Payables & Receivables	Total Year Projected	Diff. Col. 6 & Col. 8
4.	5.	6.	7.	8.	9.	10.

(B) QUARTERLY REPORT.

THIRD QUARTERLY BUDGET ANALYSIS	GROUP CARE PROGRAM Nine Months	Per cent	Budget
210 Head Teacher	25,430.00	76%	33,455
211 Asst. Teacher	17,935.56	67%	26,783
212 Teacher Aide	13,075.83	82.8%	15,787
213 Substitute	7,677.46	109.7%	7,000
230 Fringe	5,528.32	87.4%	6,324
240 Educ. Consumables	1,580.65	81.4%	1,941
250 Educ. Equipment	381.01	42.3%	900
260 Recreation	14.00	35%	40
200 CARE AND TEACHING TOTAL	71,622.83	77.7%	92,230
310 Executive Director	5,051.18	73.9%	6,837
311 Bookkeeper	2,686.33	73.9%	3,636
312 Recep./Secy.	2,070.62	75.8%	2,731
313 Adminstrative Coord.	3,474.89	78.1%	4,448
314 Program Coordinator			
315 Assistant Coordinator			
330 Fringe	1,090.93	81%	1,346
340 Office Consumable	562.10	83.5%	673
350 Office Equipment	(119.64)	0%	135
360 Telephone	554.86	72.8%	762
370 Insurance	392.23	92.9%	422
380 Public Information	60.22	89.9%	67
390 Misc. (inc. Audit)	167.84	106.9%	157
300 ADMINISTRATION TOTAL	15,991.56	75.4%	21,214
410 Nutritionist	2,776.19	72.1%	3,852
411 Cooks	4,276.61	73.3%	5,835
412 Cooks' Aides	2,507.26	108.4%	2,312
430 Nutritionist fringe	174.31		
431 Other fringe	415.58	48.3%	1,221
440 Food Costs	7,859.87	74.9%	10,500
441 Non-food consumables	351.16	43.9%	800
450 Kitchen Equipment		0%	300
400 NUTRITION TOTAL	18,360.98	74%	24,820

Chart continues on pages 82 and 83.

FUNCTIONAL PROGRAM BUDGET, WITH DEVIATION ANALYSIS.

FAMILY CARE PROGRAM			SCHOOL AGE PROGRAM		
Nine Months	Per cent	Budget	Nine Months	Per cent	Budget
66,198.85	81.2%	81,534	1,888.35	75.5%	2,500
			3,346.44	74.4%	4,500
			2,755.84	183.7%	1,500
4,121.14	72.2%	5,707	493.83	83%	595
176.09	35.2%	500	170.55	34.1%	500
37.86	76%	500		0%	500
			38.70	19.4%	200
70,533.94	79.9%	88,241	8,693.71	84.4%	10,295
5,050.92	75.1%	6,725	1,262.73	75.1%	1,681
2,686.13	75.1%	3,577	671.53	75.1%	894
2,070.39	77.1%	2,686	517.59	77%	672
3,474.72	79.4%	4,374	868.68	79.5%	1,093
7,614.98	70.8%	10,760	1,888.68	75%	2,500
5,996.25	94.3%	6,360			
2,293.88	91%	2,522	508.49	100.5%	506
758.18	121.9%	622	142.94	86.6%	165
	0%	132		0%	33
573.68	76.5%	750	159.78	85.4%	187
392.18	94.5%	415	98.59	94.8%	104
60.01	90.9%	66	14.45	85%	17
167.73	108.9%	154	41.93	107.5%	39
31,139.05	79.5%	39,183	6,175.39	78.3%	7,891
2,776.31	75.1%	3,697	694.03	89.8%	838
			58.31		
174.02	67.2%	259	47.92	81.2%	59
7,267.25	68.1%	10,668	435.89	36.3%	1,200
7.00			1.43	1%	150
10,224.58	69.9%	14,624	1,237.58	55.1%	2,247

Chart continues on pages 82 and 83.

THIRD QUARTERLY BUDGET ANALYSIS		GROUP CARE PROGRAM		
		Nine Months	Percent	Budget
510	Floor Maintenance	2,816.27	51.7%	5,783
530	Fringe	173.32		
540	Occupancy Consumables	1,123.37	126.2%	890
550	Occupancy Repair	421.74	9.5%	4,449
560	Utility	3,932.16	76.5%	5,138
570	Rent			
500	OCCUPANCY TOTAL	8,466.86	52%	16,260
610	Mental Health	455.00	91%	500
630	Medical Contract		0%	300
640	First Aid/Health	102.28	81.8%	125
600	HEALTH TOTAL	557.28	60.2%	925
710	Training	459.35	91.9%	500
740	Training supplies	10.49	10.5%	100
700	TRAINING TOTAL	469.84	78.3%	600
810	Children's Transportation	10,858.42	74.9%	14,500
840	Staff Transportation	186.00	37.2%	500
800	TRANSPORTATION TOTAL	11,044.42	73.6%	15,000
910	Social Service	2,791.27	69.1%	4,037
930	Fringe	177.19	62.6%	283
950	SOCIAL SERVICE TOTAL	2,968.46	68.7%	4,320
TOTALS		129,482.23	73.8%	175,369

FAMILY CARE PROGRAM			SCHOOL AGE PROGRAM		
Nine Months	Percent	Budget	Nine Months	Percent	Budget
281.53	52.5%	574	83.80	63.7%	143
19.98			7.22		
111.10	126.3%	88	92.43	420.1%	22
42.11	9.5%	441	249.79	227.1%	110
393.04	77.1%	510	98.24	77.4%	127
			800.00	66.7%	1,200
847.76	52.6%	1,613	1,331.48	83.1%	1,602
			25.00	12.5%	200
	0%	200			
	0%	200	3.31	3.3%	100
	0%	400	28.31	9.4%	300
			670.00	223.3%	300
3.50	1.4%	250		0%	50
3.50	1.4%	250	670.00	191.4%	350
			580.00	72.5%	800
377.16	62.9%	600			
377.16	62.9%	600	580.00	72.5%	800
2,791.01	70.3%	3,971	697.76	70.3%	993
171.14	61.6%	278	47.20	68.4%	69
2,962.15	69.7%	4,249	744.96	70.1%	1,062
116,088.14	77.8%	14,916	19,461.43	79.3%	24,547

(C) ANNUAL BUDGET REPORT AND PROJECTION

CHILD DAY CARE ASSOCIATION: 1980–1981

	1979–80	1980–81
REVENUE		
Food Reimbursement	2,885	3,200
Child Care Fees - Full-fee	44,052	88,078
Child Care Fees - DDS	32,494	
Total Revenue	79,431	91,278
EXPENSES		
Instructional		
Salaries	48,283	52,628
Substitutes	2,000	2,200
Payroll Taxes (SS + Min. Wge. up)	4,511	5,100
Supplies	2,700	3,000
Equipment	200	200
Training	150	150
Travel	150	150
Insurance	1,000	1,050
Collection Expense	100	100
Camp	350	400
Advertising	100	200
Licenses, misc.	150	200
Total Instructional	59,694	65,378
Food		
Food	3,500	4,000
Food Service/Supplies	850	850
Lunches - K + summer	3,900	4,250
Total Food	8,250	9,100
Facility		
School Use Fees $1.94 sq. ft.	3,974	4,300
Repairs	200	200
Utilities/phone	370	400
Total Facility	4,544	4,900
Transportation	1,800	2,000
MCDCA Administration	6,200	6,700
TOTAL CENTER	80,488	88,078

PROPOSED FEES Beginning School Year: $263 per month B + A Kindergarten
220 " After Kindergarten
178 " B + A School
153 " After School

The extra revenue is to build our reserve which we must have to cover 2 payrolls.

(B) The second form is a quarterly report—a program budget organized by function, with a deviation analysis. This director who runs a day care center with a satellite family day care system, and a school-age day care program, finds it useful to compare expenditures by function and across programs.

(C) The third form is a report of income and expenses for the year ending, and a projected plan for the year to come, using an income and expense form, and two columns. This form is used to explain the reasons for a change in fees. It gives figures for a very small program for school-age children that is provided in school space.

9. MONITORING AND ACCOUNTING FOR EXPENDITURES AND INCOME

All the above budget tools are primarily management tools. They give you signals when expenditures begin to exceed income. It is not enough just to be able to put together a budget; it must be used, and used quickly when action is needed.

For a not-for-profit center, the board must be persuaded to act instantly on negative information about the state of finances at the center. Attendance records, fee collection records, cash flow projections, break-even analysis, and all these forms are a way of compiling and producing information which must lead to action by a board, or by an owner or director. If one side of a budget changes the other side must be changed to match, or action taken to correct the initial change. In day care the action needs to be immediate. Facing facts before they engulf you is important.

Many organizations fail to act on early symptoms of financial trouble when they might be able to correct the problem easily. With every week that goes by, the problem becomes cumulatively more serious until finally, when there is not any way to avoid the problem any more, the indebtedness is very serious. Day care programs have so little cash that they can seldom afford to wait for a problem to become a crisis.

The most important control on expenditures is the accounting system which provides the information about how the money is being spent. This manual does not attempt to present accounting skills, since it is likely that the center will employ an accountant or an accountant service.

However, for your use, a basic set of concepts is reprinted in this book on the following pages from *A People's Guide to Accounting,* developed by Jon Atkinson of the Massachusetts Office for Children.

Excellent material is also available from the Grantsmanship Center, 1015 West Olympic Boulevard, Los Angeles, California 90015, on accounting, budgeting, proposal writing, public relations, grants, and public funding.

Accounting is a major tool for controlling expenditures, by providing the information you need on what is being spent. All day care programs need such accounting, either through employing their own bookkeeper/accountant; employing an outside accountant; or purchasing computerized accounting services from a bank or computer service firm. Accounting services are a necessity of day care life.

In addition, there are a number of small, practical steps which a small organization can institute, and which a large organization must institute, to minimize the risk of misuse of funds, embezzlement, or theft. An employer should never be so lax in procedures that employees are presented with easy temptations that could destroy their lives.

One expert[1] outlines twelve controls in detail:

1. Use prenumbered receipts for all fees and other cash income.

2. Collection of cash should be under the control of two people when possible.

3. If checks come in the mail, two people should open the mail.

4. All income should be deposited at once in the bank, and none of it should ever be used to pay bills or make purchases.

5. All disbursements except petty cash should be made by check, and no check should be written by the bookkeeper unless there is supporting documentation or approval.

6. If the check signer is also the bookkeeper, two signatures should be required on all checks.

7. A person other than the bookkeeper should receive bank statements and reconcile them.

8. Someone other than the bookkeeper should be the one to authorize writing off of accounts receivable or other assets.

9. Marketable securities should be kept in the bank.

10. Records of assets should be kept, and inventories made periodically.

11. Excess cash should be maintained in a separate bank account requiring two signatures.

12. Fidelity insurance should be carried.

---

[1] Malvern Gross, *Financial and Accounting Guide for Nonprofit Organizations,* New York, Ronald Press, 1974.

10. Meeting Tax and Other Government Obligations

The day care organization is required to file the following forms for the federal government, as applicable:

IRS 1023 or 1024, for tax exemption as a 501 (c) 3 or 501 (c) 4 corporation

IRS Form SS-4 Employer Identification Number for tax exempt organization

US Postal Office, application for postal permit for bulk mailing

US Department of Labor, "Significant Provisions of State Unemployment Insurance Law," prepared by Employment and Training Administration Unemployment Insurance Service, probably also available from State Employment Security Agency

Local District Office of the IRS, procedures and forms for the Federal Insurance Contributions Act (FICA tax)

IRS Form W-4, federal withholding tax certificates for employees

IRS Form 941, which must be filed *quarterly,* the employee withholding tax return

IRS Form 990, annual federal tax return for tax exempt organizations

1040 Schedule C, tax return for day care organizations, not tax exempt

1099 IRS Form, if you paid more than $600 to a consultant

See federal publications which can be helpful in filing these forms:

Publication # 557—How to Apply for an Exemption
Publication # 15—Employer's Tax Guide Circular E
Publication # 393—Federal Employment Tax Forms

From the state government, you will need the following forms:

Application form for state day care license

Forms for Workmen's Compensation and State Unemployment Insurance from State Employment Security Office

Forms for annual report for incorporated organizations

Forms for reporting child abuse, at Child Protection Unit, Welfare Department (or Department of Family and Children's Services)

In addition, you will want the forms for applying for funds, such as Title XX or child protection.

It is a good idea to keep copies of all these forms, along with relevant codes and laws, in a notebook, kept up to date.

11. PROTECTING THE CENTER THROUGH INSURANCE

There are many potential expenses of a day care program which could be incurred through a loss caused by fire, theft, or other disaster; through vehicle collision, through accident to children, or damage to parents, through costs of legal defense against suits, or loss of suits; through breach of contract, or through torts. An extremely useful resource is the *Legal Handbook for Day Care Centers* by William Aikman, Lawrence Kotin, and Robert Crabtree.

Aikman suggests focusing on two things in thinking through whether the cost of insurance is worth the value received: the degree of potential risk, and the amount in dollars of potential loss. In each case, the alternative might be to be self-insured; that is, to gamble that the risk will be small, or, if the unfortunate event happens, the financial liability is not great.

For example, if the center is uninsured against collision, an accident would probably not bankrupt the center. On the other hand, an uninsured personal injury liability could bankrupt the center easily.

The most important types of insurance coverage which *are often required* are liability insurance, vehicle insurance, Workmen's Compensation, and fidelity bonding. The most important types of insurance as employee benefits are Blue Cross/Blue Shield and other health plans, retirement plans, and Social Security (FICA which is required once the center makes the initial decision to participate).

Liability insurance protects you against the consequence of "negligence." Most liability policies cover: accidental bodily injury; accidental damage to another person's property; expenses of immediate medical relief at the time of the accident; cost of legal defense against suits. Although $300,000 might be considered reasonable insurance, the potential financial liability is very great, so that some centers carry insurance up to $1,000,000. For food prepared by the day care program you may want additional coverage up to $300,000 if that liability not included in the other policy. Personal property of $5000 or more should be insured separately, if not in the policy.

Vehicle insurance is required in many states. Automobile liability insurance is a high priority for day care programs. When a center permits staff to transport children in their personal cars, it is essential that the additional liability insurance be provided. For example, a center might pay the staff person to increase the coverage to a higher level on her own automobile insurance policy. Or it is possible that the center's vehicle policy or general liability policy could include a rider to cover this use.

Fire insurance is standardized throughout the United States. It covers only fire, lightning, and losses to goods connected with the fire. Rates are based on construction material, nearness to fire protection services, and property value. "Extended coverage options" extends coverage to smoke damage.

Theft insurance may be combined with fire, or may be purchased separately. In high crime areas, theft insurance may be very expensive or even unobtainable. Federal Crime Insurance is available in such urban areas from regular insurance agents.

Children's insurance covers the cost of medical services for children resulting from injuries or accidents while they are in the care of the center, including field trips provided by the center. The insurance is very inexpensive, and is often paid for by parents. It pays on the basis of the injury, without determining negligence.

Fidelity bonding. The director, bookkeeper, or treasurer are sometimes bonded to safeguard against embezzlement.

Indemnification insurance is available to protect against personal liability of board members. However, at present board members are usually not personally liable, and the available insurance does not protect against the more dangerous forms of board liability. This type of insurance is not at present a good buy. Training of board members in their responsibilities and potential liabilities is a better course.

Workmen's Compensation is required in many states, if there are ten or more employees. Whether insured or not, an employer is liable. He is required to provide employees a safe place to work, hire competent fellow employees, provide safe tools, and warn employees of existing dangers. Workmen's

Compensation insurance pays medical costs and work time lost beyond seven days because of accidents or injuries at work. Because of the potential liability, this type of insurance is useful protection even if it is not required.

Unemployment insurance protects workers who are laid off and cannot find employment. Unemployment benefits are a right of all employees. The amount of benefits received and the length of time they are paid are determined by state law. If a laid-off employee claims unemployment, the center must pay its share, which is a continuing cost to the center as long as the person is not re-employed. If a person is laid off from a day care program and finds a job in another organization not covered, or stays there only a small amount of time, the day care center will be responsible for some of the unemployment insurance.

Social Security is more of a tax than an insurance plan. A not-for-profit organization just starting has a choice of whether or not to participate. Because of the benefits to employees, it is desirable to participate. Employers contribute 6.7% of wages of their staff. See "Your Social Security" published by the U.S. Department of Health, Education and Welfare, Social Security Administration, January 1976 (DHEW SSA 76-10035).

Health insurance generally covers either hospital, surgical, and medical, or major medical expenses. Group policies at the place of employment generally lower the cost to the individual and are important employee fringe benefits. Day care programs themselves can get insurance as part of a group plan, for example as members of the Day Care Council of America.

Life insurance, disability insurance, dental insurance, and pension plans are usually beyond the budget capacity of many day care programs to provide as fringe benefits for their employees even on a cost-sharing basis. Those centers can, however, make such insurance available through a group plan as a service to their employees.

Glossary of Terms used in Banking and in Day Care Financial Management

"Acid test" ratio Cash plus any other assets that can be converted to cash *immediately* should equal or be greater than current liabilities. The formula used is the following:

$$\frac{\text{cash} + \text{receivables (net)} + \text{marketable assets}}{\text{current liabilities}}$$

The "acid test" ratio is one of the common barometers used by banks in extending credit, because it indicates the ability of an organization to meet its obligations.

Accounts receivable or "receivables" All the items in which some other person or organization owes money to you that has not yet been paid. "Aging receivables" is a term describing a scheduling of accounts receivable according to the length of time they have been outstanding. This shows which accounts are not being paid in a timely manner, and may reveal problems with accounts not easily collected.

Amortization The process of gradually paying off a liability on the installment plan over a period of time.

Assets The valuable resources, tangible property, and property rights owned by an individual or an organization.

Attendance The number of children who actually came to the day care program on a particular day, or during a particular week, month, or year.

Bad debts Accounts receivable which will never be collected.

Balance sheet An itemized statement which lists the total assets and the total liabilities of an organization to portray its net worth at a given moment in time.

Break-even analysis A method used to determine or portray the point at which an organization will neither make a profit nor incur a loss. At this point the total dollars coming in will exactly offset the cost of providing the service to the number of children using it.

Budget   A plan for a given period of time, itemized by categories of expenditures, of all the money that will be spent, and an itemizing, by sources of revenues, of all the money that is expected to be paid in.

Budget justification   A detailed narrative that explains why each item in the budget is determined at that particular amount.

Capital equipment   Equipment costing you more than $250 which you will use over a period of a number of years rather than using it up in one year.

Cash flow   The actual movement of cash to operate the day care program: cash inflow compared with cash outflow. Used to offer a better indication of the ability of an organization to meet its own obligations than the conventional net income figure shown on an income and expense statement.

Cash position   See liquidity.

Collateral   Property, stocks, bonds, savings accounts, life insurance, and current assets, any or all of which may be held or offered to insure repayment of a loan.

Contract   A legally binding agreement, whether written or oral, entered into by two parties. To be legally enforceable, a contract must have something offered, accepted by another party, and an agreed on "consideration." The consideration can be money that the person agrees to pay for the thing offered, or it can be anything else of value, such as free child care in exchange for cleaning services.

Cooperative   A form of organization, either for-profit or not-for-profit, that shares assets with contributing members.

Corporation   An artificial "person" or legal entity created under government laws and given certain powers and responsibilities; a group of individuals or legal entities that voluntarily join together under the law to form a for-profit or a not-for-profit enterprise.

Costs   All the resources expended to produce the service in the program, including money, the value of things, and the value of time spent by individuals. Costs include the following:

> *Cash costs*   All the out-of-pocket expenses in money, whether paid by check or money.

> *In-kind costs*   All the donated time of individuals who volunteer or work overtime without receiving pay; contributions in staff time from other agencies.

92

True costs All the costs, both in-kind and cash.

Variable costs All the costs that are dependent on the number of children in the program, and differ at different numbers of children.

Fixed costs All the costs that are the same even when the numbers of children vary.

Current assets Cash or other items that will normally be turned into cash within one year, and assets that will be used up in the normal operations of the program within one year, but are presently on hand.

Current liabilities Amounts owed that will ordinarily be paid within one year. Such items include all accounts payable, wages payable, taxes payable, the current portion of a long-term debt, and interest payments.

Current ratio A ratio of a firm's current assets to its current liabilities.

Depreciation A reduction in the value of an asset over time. The most important causes of depreciation are wear and tear, and gradual obsolescence. For-profit organizations use a bookkeeping charge for depreciation to write off the original cost of the asset, less expected salvage value, by equitably distributing charges against operations over its entire useful life. Small not-for-profit organizations, that have no tax advantage from depreciation, often simplify their bookkeeping by replacing assets on a rotating schedule and ignoring depreciation charges.

Deviation The difference between planned expenditures or income and actual expenditures or income, expressed either in amounts (dollars) or percentages.

Enrollment The number of children whose parents have agreed to send them to the day care program in a given period of time.

Entrepreneur An innovator who recognizes opportunities and who mobilizes the necessary resources, engages in the necessary planning, and organizes the factors needed to organize the service in order to use the perceived opportunity to create a reality of new service.

Equity The monetary value of a property or an enterprise which is greater than the claims against it held by others.

Fees The price decided upon for the service (see sliding fees), to be paid by parents or by government or a combination, for each child.

Fringe benefits   All the money and in-kind insurance, vacations, and other benefits offered to a staff person over and above his or her wages. Fringe benefits include employer share of taxes, FICA, Workmen's Compensation, bonding, health and retirement plans, paid training, and paid recreational programs.

FTE or Full Time Equivalent   The number of full time children or staff that would result if part time children or staff were added together. Example: 3 Monday-Wednesday-and-Friday children and three Tuesday-and-Thursday children together are 3 FTE children.

Functional cost categories   The use of uniform categories of costs related to different functions of a day care program enables costs to be compared from one program to another. In day care, standard functions have been identified as follows: care and teaching, social services, food services, health services, staff development, administration, occupancy, and transportation. The first five are functions performed, and the last three are supporting functions.

Illiquid   See liquidity.

Income and expense statement   Same as a Profit and Loss Statement, or an Income Statement. An itemized list of all income and all expenses for a given period of time. Income statements that are cast into the future are called *income projections,* and are forecasting and budget tools estimating income and anticipating expenditures to come.

Liquidity   A term used to describe solvency, particularly of a for-profit business, and which has special reference to the degree to which assets can be readily converted into cash without a loss. Also called **Cash position.** If an organization's current assets cannot be converted into cash to meet its liabilities, it is said to be **illiquid.**

Long-term liabilities   These are expenses which are incurred but which will not mature within the current year.

Market   The number of people and their spending of money, actual or potential, for day care within the geographic area you serve. Families that do not need day care, or that can find it within their family without paying money for it, are not in the market.

Market share   The percent of the market that you serve, as compared with other similar day care services in the geographic area.

Net worth   The owner's equity in a proprietary business, represented by the excess of total assets over amounts owed (liabilities) at a given moment. Also the net worth of an individual or a corporation as determined by deducting the amount of personal or corporate liabilities from the total value of personal or corporate assets.

Occupancy costs   All expenditures for rent or mortgage payments, utilities, maintenance, and other costs associated with the physical facility.

Partnership   A legal relationship created voluntarily by two or more persons who associate together as co-owners of a business for profit.

Payables or accounts payable   All the money you owe someone else at a given time, which is due to be paid.

Pro forma   A projection or estimate of what may result in the future from actions in the present. A *pro forma* financial statement is one that projects how the operations of the organization will turn out if certain assumptions come true.

Profit   The excess of revenues coming in after all costs and expenses incurred are paid. A **for-profit** organization is one that is either a proprietorship, corporation, partnership, or cooperative that anticipates that such an excess will exist, although in reality it may not. A **not-for-profit** corporation is a legal entity that is created in the anticipation that it will break even, and will use any excess revenues within the program. A for-profit organization may use profit to distribute to investors, but a not-for-profit organization may not.

Profit and loss statement   See **Income and expense statement**.

Program budget   When a single agency or organization runs more than one program, a way of presenting financial information that identifies the costs of each program—rather than lumping them together in combined items—so that the costs of programs can be compared and analyzed.

Proprietorship or sole proprietorship   A type of business organization in which one individual owns the business. Legally, the owner *is* the business, and personal assets are exposed to any liabilities of the business.

Slot   A space that can be filled for a child in a day care program. Financial management in day care projects and budgets for a number of slots, and collects fees for each child filling a slot. Over the course of a budget year, a single slot could be occupied by several children in succession. Similarly, a slot could be filled by different children coming different days, or parts of days.

Start-up costs   One-time-only costs that are incurred in the period before a day care program is operating at its budgeted capacity, and including the costs of operating below an efficient level before the full number of children has been recruited and enrolled and has paid fees. **Operating costs,** in contrast, are the costs of running a program after the start-up period is over and the program is operating in an annual budget cycle.

Sliding fee   A schedule of fees that varies according to ability to pay.

Tax deduction   An expenditure that is a legitimate cost of doing business or is allowed by the IRS to be deducted (as in the case of charitable gifts), that in combination will be subtracted from the amount earned in figuring taxes owed on profit. Employers may deduct their contributions for day care from their taxable income.

Tax credit   An amount that is subtracted, not from taxable income, but from the amount of tax owed, or the tax bill. Parents get a credit of 20% to 30% on their personal income tax, which means that after figuring the tax owed the government on their income less deductible expenditures, they can then subtract from that bill a percentage of their total child care expenditures.

Target market   The specific families, characterized by socioeconomic, demographic, and/or interest characteristics, who are identified as potential users of a day care service.

Utilization   A factor based on the past relationship between enrollment expectation and actual enrollment that allows for the fact that there are lags between one child leaving a slot and its being filled with another child.

Working capital, net   An excess of current assets over current liabilities that permits money to be available for carrying on the operations and cushioning cash flow problems.

Useful Resources

Abt Associates, 55 Wheeler Street, Cambridge, MA 02138, *Children at the Center* and *Day Care Centers in the U.S.*

Bangs, David H., Jr. and Osgood, William R. *Business Planning Guide.* The Federal Reserve Bank of Boston, 1976.

Child Welfare League of America, 67 Irving Place, New York, NY 10003 Boguslawski, D. B. *Guide for Establishing and Operating Day Care Centers for Young Children,* revised 1975.

Grantsmanship Center, 1015 West Olympic Boulevard, Los Angeles, CA 90015. Large number of useful reprints on fund-raising and financial management including:
A Guide to Public Relations
Program Planning and Proposal Writing
Guide to Accounting for Nonprofits

Gross, Malvern. *Financial and Accounting Guide for Nonprofit Organizations.* New York: Ronald Press, 1974.

Host, Malcolm, *Day Care Administration.* Washington, D.C.: DHEW, 1971.

Lasser, J. K., *Accounting for Everyday Profit.* Larchmont, NY: New York University Press, 1957.

Lurie, Robert, *Making Child Care Work: Managing for Quality.* Resources for Child Care Management, P.O. Box 669, Summit, NJ 07901. 1985.

Rowe, Mary P. "The Costs of Child Care: Money and Other Resources," Chapter Eight in Massachusetts Early Education Project, *Child Care in Massachusetts, the Public Responsibility,* 1971, reprinted DCCDCA, 1972.

Save the Children Child Care Support Center, 1182 West Peachtree Street, N.W., Atlanta, GA 30309.
Day Care Financial Management, 1981.
Recruiting and Enrolling Children, 1981.

The most useful accounting manual: "Dollars and Sense," now available from National Technical Information Service, 5285 Port Royal Road, Springfield, VA 22161 for $14.50 ($4.50 microfiche).

The most useful legal manual: *Legal Handbook for Day Care Centers,* by William Aikman, Lawrence Kotin, and Robert Crabtree, now available from Government Printing Office, Washington, D.C., and from federal bookstores for $7.50.

Other Sources of Information

Child Care Information Exchange is a magazine for day care directors, published and edited by Roger Neugebauer, C-44, Redmond, WA 98052, (206)882-1066.

The Internal Revenue Service has valuable publications. See Publication Number 534, *Depreciation.* Many libraries have reference sets of IRS publications which you can read or copy.

Small Business Administration, with offices throughout the United States, offers publications, training sessions, and loans for the small, for-profit business. There is also a program in which retired businessmen offer expert help to small for-profit businesses.

American Institute of Certified Public Accountants (AICPA), 666 Fifth Avenue, New York, NY 10019, (212)581-8840. Contact: Manager, Accounting Aid Program. This organization may be able to locate free accountant assistance for needy programs.

National Association of Accountants, 919 Third Avenue, New York, NY 10022, (212)371-9124. Contact: Manager, Socioeconomic Programs. Another possible source of donated accountant help.

A guide to double-entry bookkeeping, *Effective Fiscal Management in Human Services Programs, Volume Two, Guide to Bookkeeping,* can be obtained by writing Madeline Dowling, Division of Research and Demonstration, Office of Program Development, OHDS, US DHHS, Room 716E Humphrey, 200 Independence Ave. SW, Washington, DC 20201, (202)245-6233.

Resources for Child Care Management provides educational conferences in your local area, publishes materials, offers management expertise to the child care industry, and starts and manages high quality child care services. For further information write Resources, P.O. Box 669, Summit, NJ 07901, or call (201)277-2689.

If there is a child care resource and referral center in your area, these are excellent sources of help and assistance to the day care field.

APPENDIX
People's Guide to Day Care Accounting

This material was prepared by Jonathan Atkinson for the Governor's Advisory Committee on Child Development in Massachusetts. It was first published in 1973, and has been distributed by the Massachusetts Office for Children.

This section sets forth basic accounting principles specifically useful to day care. At the outset, let us mention two accounting problems which particularly face day care providers:

1. *Institutional Funding Sources*—If you receive money from the Department of Public Welfare, United Community Services, Office for Children, Headstart, Community Development, etc., (which a large number of day care operators do), you will be required to present some kind of periodic financial report designed by these funding organizations for their use. In this case, your accounting system must be able to satisfy these requirements, or you'll have some problems. (Funding sources can help by standardizing their reporting requirements, but that's not yet accomplished.) In any event, day care accounting has the particular problem of furnishing reports to funding sources.

2. *"In-kind contributions"*—Many day care providers get staff time from volunteers; free or reduced rental rates for space; contributions of material, supplies, food; even consultant help, *none* of which involve a cash transaction. The question is: should your accounting system make room for these non-monetary transactions? (Answers to come later.)
   Like any business, day care accounting serves by keeping a record of:
   a) how much money you spend
   b) how much money you receive
   c) what you spend your money on
   d) where you receive your money from
This simple function of accounting must not be lost, especially when you get involved in all the technical aspects. *Accounting serves you by keeping a record.*
   In business, accounting records ultimately measure financial profits and growth (or loss and contraction). Aside from our natural propensity to count things, this is the basic reason why "accounting" came into business in the first place.
   Day care, however, is a slightly different case. The essential reason for the existence of most day care centers is to participate, help, and watch

99

children grow, learn, and live. Most often, financial profit and growth are only a by-product of day care, not the *raison d'etre*. (Note: Of the approximate 1,200 centers and family day care systems in Massachusetts, nearly half are non-profit organizations. Nearly all of the remaining "profit-making" day care services are delivered by small, family-run, "mom and pop" organizations.)[1]

In any event, the incentive to "account" in day care is a little different from what it is in standard business activity. Still there are incentives to keep clear books:

> so you'll know if you have enough money to keep operating
>
> so you can pay your staff on time
>
> so you have some idea what expenses will face you next year or next month
>
> so you can prepare clear, useful reports

Even if you don't make money, it's easier and more fun if things run smoothly.

Basically it's up to you how you set up your accounting system. If your bookkeeper or secretary is not comfortable with what books are before him or her, then the system is no good. There are many actual ways of keeping accounts. They're all good, if the people who use them are happy with them.

If there's one general fault I've found, it's that some ways for accounting are more complicated than necessary. Keep your system simple. Let it serve you, not the other way around.

Planning Beforehand

If you are starting a day care program, or planning day care services, you have some freedom. Spend time thinking beforehand to avoid headaches later.

Think about what services you are going to provide. This will serve as the basis for your accounts. Under the category of "Services" come staff, whether salaried or consulting, food, supplies, space, insurance, benefits, transportation, and specialized services that your program provides.

Next, think about where you are going to get your money. Will fees be supplemented by contracts, grants, or income from properties? What kinds of "in-kind" contributions are you counting on? Be as thorough and far-sighted in your list as you can be.

Accounting Cornerposts

Now that you've got at least a skeletal notion of your operation, it's time to learn the cornerposts of accounting. They are:

---

1. *Where are We? Where Are We Going? Facts on Day Care in Massachusetts*, rev. ed. (Massachusetts Governor's Advisory Council on Child Development, 1973).

Journal
Ledger
"Double Entry"
Balance Sheet

Many accounting books start off by presenting your balance sheet first. However, I feel day care lends itself better to presenting the "working" tools first, i.e., the journal and ledger.

The Journal. In this day and age of ultrasophisticated digital data retrieval systems (i.e., computers), the most disarmingly simple accounting system I've seen in day care was something that looked like a big check book. In fact, the people at this small center ran it like you do with your check book at home, the exception being that a certified public accountant would come in at the end of each year, check the adding, and produce a year-end statement. I'd say, if you can keep a check book, then you can start a day care center (assuming you know how to help children to grow and learn.)

The reason this story is germane here is that a journal is essentially your check-book operation. The official definition goes something like this:

> *Journal: Book of original entry. A chronological record of each transaction your day care center makes, including date, description of transaction, amount, special explanation if needed, and debit and credit entry designating the proper account.*

In other words, anything that affects the financial status of your program must appear in a "journal." For our purposes, it's the starting point. Here is a picture of a journal:

A.B.C. DAY CARE, INC.

	Date 1982	Explanation	Acct #	Debit	Credit
1	Jul 6	deposited CASH IN BANK	04	700 —	
2		from PARENT FEES	09		700 —
3	10	deposited CASH IN BANK	04	1000 —	
4		from CONTRACT w/D.P.W.	10		1000 —
5	22	bought ADMIN SUPPLIES	15	75 —	
6		paid from CASH IN BANK	04		75 —
7	27	paid SALARIES	12	900 —	
8		from CASH IN BANK	04		900 —
9	27	paid RENT for Aug.	13	400 —	
10		from CASH IN BANK	04		400 —
11					

Now let's just say right here not to get worried about debit or credit. That will be clarified very soon, so keep reading.

The Ledger.   At the most detailed extreme, each and every transaction you make can have a separate account. The series of these accounts is called the Ledger. At a minimum, every general category of financial transaction needs to have an account.

Think of each of your Journal transactions as taking some eggs from one basket and putting them in another (instead of eggs, of course, they're dollars). Well, the baskets are your accounts and all the baskets lined up in a row is your Ledger.

Ledger: The series of accounts which describe your operation.

CASH IN BANK — 04

	Debit		Credit	
Jul 6		700 —	Jul 22	75 —
10		1000 —	27	900 —
			27	400 —

REVENUE FROM FEES — 09

	Debit		Credit	
		Jul 6		700 —

SALARY EXPENSES — 12

	Debit		Credit
Jul 27	900 —		

RENT EXPENSES — 13

	Debit		Credit
Jul 27	400 —		

How you set up your accounts within your ledger depends on your own needs and desires, but also on what reports may be required of you if you get monies from funding organizations. You want your accounts to match what reports you have to submit; it makes your work easier. It's useful to think about this before setting up your separate accounts.

Double Entry: Debit and Credit. Every accounting book has a sentence like this: "The purpose served by the words 'debit and credit' might just as well be served by the words 'left' and 'right'." Well, I wish they had. I think it would make things simpler. But no bona fide accountant is going to talk with you without debit and credit entering in.

Double entry, in which every transaction is entered twice, left and right, is a way of recording the two sides of a business transaction: taking something out in order to put it in elsewhere. In essence, if you receive something, you must get it from somewhere. And once you get it, you have to put it somewhere.

Parents' pocketbook

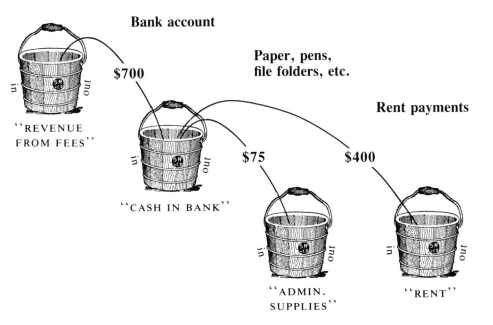

Bank account

Paper, pens, file folders, etc.

Rent payments

$700

$75 $400

in   out
"REVENUE FROM FEES"

in   out
"CASH IN BANK"

in   out
"ADMIN. SUPPLIES"

in   out
"RENT"

Each account, then, has a left and right which serve as your "in" and "out". One side is for everything you put in an account; the other side is what you take out.

Now, there are certain classifications for accounts (made clear when we get to the balance sheet.) which affect whether you call the "in" a debit or credit. Here is a little chart:

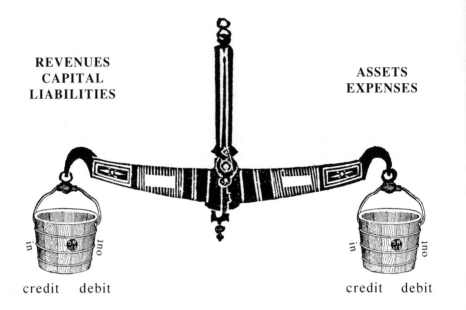

REVENUES
CAPITAL
LIABILITIES

ASSETS
EXPENSES

credit   debit

credit   debit

RESOURCES FROM
THEIR BUCKET

RESOURCES INTO
AND FROM YOUR BUCKET

Rather than trying to give a rationale for why this is (which would be long and not necessarily clear) I think at this point it would serve you better to say that this is the way it is, in accordance with "standard practice."

The Balance Sheet. A balance sheet essentially shows where you are financially at the end of a given time period. The time period can be a week, or a month, but it's most typically a year. A balance sheet also always balances (or should if your adding is right), and says: Assets = Liabilities plus Capital.

A.B.C. DAY CARE, INC.

Balance Sheet

Period ending _____
(date)

ASSETS

Cash		_____
Accounts Receivable		_____
Inventory		_____
Equipment	_____	
Less: Depreciation	_____	_____
Prepaid Expenses		_____
Total Assets		_____

LIABILITIES & CAPITAL

Accounts Payable	_____
Notes Payable	_____
Accrued Expenses Payable	_____
Total Liabilities	_____
Capital Stock	_____
Surplus	_____
Total Liabilities & Capital	_____

Note: Balance sheet can also be set up side by side, with liabilities and capital on the left.

While year-end balance sheets may be important to day care operations, certain fiscal reports may be handier. A report which balances how much you spent (in all of your different accounts) with what revenues you took in, will serve better for future planning. Here is an example report which is like a balance sheet, but perhaps more helpful to day care operation.

A VALUABLE REPORT FORM

(Monthly, Quarterly, or Yearly)

COSTS	Check one or both	Cash	In-kind	$ expended this period _____	Total $ expended to date	Projected expense next: _____
SALARIES & CONSULTANTS						
Care and teaching						
Administrative						
Food						
Health						
Social Service						
Transportation						
Maintenance						
FRINGE BENEFITS						
TRAINING, STAFF DEVELOPMENT						
MATERIALS, SUPPLIES						
Food						
Child Related						
Administrative						
Other						
EQUIPMENT						
Child Related						
Administration						
RENOVATION, REPAIRS						
SPACE COST						
TRANSPORTATION COST						
GRAND TOTAL						
NET CASH IN BANK						

REVENUES (CASH & IN-KIND)

	Revenues this period	Total revenues to date	Projected revenues next: _____
CASH			
Fees			
Income from Service Contracts			
A.			
B.			
C.			
Other Cash Income			
A.			
B.			
IN-KIND: List Sources			
A.			
B.			
C.			
GRAND TOTAL			

An Example: Going Through the Steps

At this point a simple example will clarify how all these pieces fit together to form a whole picture of your operation.

JOURNAL A.B.C. DAY CARE: OPERATION FOR JULY

#	Date		Account		Debit	Credit
1	Jul	6	CASH IN BANK	04	700 —	
2			from PARENT FEES	09		700 —
3		10	CASH IN BANK	04	1000 —	
4			from D.P.W CONTRACT	10		1000 —
5		22	ADMIN. SUPPLIES	15	75 —	
6			from CASH IN BANK	04		75 —
7		27	SALARIES	12	900 —	
8			from CASH IN BANK	04		900 —
9		27	RENT	13	400 —	
10			from CASH IN BANK	04		400 —
11		28	TEACHING CONTRIBUTION	16	600 —	
12			from IN-KIND	11		600 —
13		31	EQUIPMENT: roof shingles	17	200 —	
14			from CASH IN BANK	04		200 —
15		31	LABOR CONTRIBUTION	18	70 —	
16			from IN-KIND	11		70 —

(note: a separate journal may be kept for in-kind entries.)

LEDGER

Parent Fees

debit	credit
	Jul 6 700

Cash in Bank

debit	credit
Jul 6 700	Jul 22 75
10 1000	27 900
	27 400
	31 200

Contract Revenues

debit	credit
	Jul 10 1000

Salary Expense

debit	credit
Jul 27 900	

In-Kind "Revenues"

debit	credit
	Jul 28 600
	31 70

Admin. Supplies

debit	credit
Jul 22 75	

Rent Expense

debit	credit
Jul 27 400	

Teaching Contribution

debit	credit
Jul 28 600	

Labor Contribution

debit	credit
Jul 31 70	

Equipment

debit	credit
Jul 31 200	

MONTHLY REPORT

Revenues:

Parent Fees	700		
DPW Contract	1000		
In-kind	670		
	2370		

Expenses:

Teaching: Salaries and In-kind	1500
Supplies & Equipment	275
Rent	400
Labor: In-kind	70
	2245
Net Cash in Bank	125
	2370

MODEL DAY CARE

CHART OF ACCOUNTS

Developed by Norman Herbert for the University of Michigan School of Education training program for day care directors compiled by Pearl G. Axelrod.

Account Number	Account Name
	ASSETS AND LIABILITIES
100.0	Cash
110.0	Utility Deposits
120.0	Buildings
121.0	Accumulated Depreciation—Buildings
123.0	Major Building Improvements
124.0	Accumulated Depreciation—Improvements
130.0	Land
140.0	Major Equipment
141.0	Accumulated Depreciation—Equipment
211.0	Income Taxes Payable—Federal
212.0	Income Taxes Payable—State
214.0	Taxes Payable—FICA Withheld
216.0	Health Insurance Payable—Withheld
217.0	Life and Accident Insurance—Withheld
218.0	Retirement—Withheld
250.0	Loans Payable
270.0	Mortgage Principal—Payable

Account Number	Account Name
530.7	Administrative
530.8	Janitor
535.8	Mortgage Interest Expense
535.8	Rent
545.0	Depreciation
545.1	Classroom Equipment
545.5	Kitchen Equipment
545.8	Building
545.85	Building Equipment
545.9	Transportation Vehicle
556.0	Licenses and Fees
560.0	Insurance
560.1	Education & Supervision
560.5	Food Services
560.7	Administration Service
560.8	Janitor
560.9	Transportation
565.0	Professional Fees

| 300.0 | Retained Earnings |
| 301.0 | Contributed Equity |

REVENUE—INCOME

400.0	Tuition
401.0	Registration Revenue
410.0	Donations
420.0	Food Reimbursement
430.0	Government Grants
440.0	Fund Raising Activities
460.0	Work Study Reimbursement
480.0	Miscellaneous

EXPENSES

500.0	Salaries Expense
500.1	Teaching Salaries
500.5	Kitchen Salaries
500.7	Administration Salaries
500.8	Janitor Salaries
500.9	Transportation Salaries
510.0	Repairs and Maintenance
510.1	Classroom Equipment & Repair
510.5	Kitchen
510.8	Building & Grounds
530.0	Payroll Taxes
530.1	Teachers
530.5	Kitchen
565.1	Education & Supervision
565.2	Special Services
565.3	Staff Development
565.4	Health Services
570.7	Telephone
572.8	Utilities (Gas, Electric, Water)
575.0	Supplies
575.1	Education & Supervision
575.3	Staff Development
575.4	Health Services
575.5	Food Services
575.6	Parent & Community Services
575.7	Administration Service
575.8	Building Occupancy
575.9	Transportation
580.0	Equipment
580.1	Education and Supervision
580.4	Health Services
580.5	Food Services
580.7	Administration Services
580.8	Building
580.9	Transportation
585.5	Food
590.9	Travel Expenses
595	Miscellaneous
600	Revenue and Expense